Seeing Your Life Through New Eyes

PAUL BRENNER, M.D., PH.D.

DONNA MARTIN, M.A.

Seeing Your Life Through New Eyes

InSights to Freedom from Your Past

BEYOND
WORDS
Publishing

Beyond Words Publishing, Inc.
20827 N.W. Cornell Road, Suite 500
Hillsboro, Oregon 97124-9808
503-531-8700
1-800-284-9673

Editor Rosemary Wray
Copyeditor/Proofreader David Abel
Design Principia Graphica
Composition William H. Brunson Typography Services
Managing editor Kathy Matthews

Printed in the United States of America
Distributed to the book trade by Publishers Group West

Library of Congress Cataloging-in-Publication Data
Brenner, Paul.
    Seeing your life through new eyes : InSights to freedom from your
past / Paul Brenner and Donna Martin.
        p. cm.
    Includes bibliographical references.
    ISBN 1-58270-022-2 (pbk.)
        1. Family—Psychological aspects.   2. Adult children of
dysfunctional families — Mental health.   3. Interpersonal relations.
4. Parent and child.   5. Self-help techniques.   I. Martin, Donna.
II. Title.

    RC455.4.F3 B74   2000
    158.2—dc21   99-088573

The corporate mission of Beyond Words Publishing, Inc.:
    Inspire to Integrity

To our parents and children,

to our families, to our ancestors—

and to those yet unborn.

Contents

Acknowledgments

Seeing Your Life Through New Eyes describes a process based on personal experience, inspiration, and many years of research with clients. We owe our patients and teachers a huge "thank you." Having recently reviewed the works of great thinkers and explorers of the psyche, from Freud to Adler and Maslow, Rogers to Hillman and Wilbur, we can see that this process (and the underlying ideas supporting it) rests on the shoulders of these and other pioneers. We are also appreciative of poets—such as Rumi, the thirteenth-century Sufi—and the other writers quoted throughout this book. (For the sources of the quotations, and for full citations of the sources mentioned in the footnotes, please consult the References section that begins on page 163.)

We owe a special thanks to Rita Falk, who contributed her thoughts, her time, and her computer wisdom to this work; to Dr. Doug Jack for his excellent suggestions; to our editors Kathy Matthews and

Rosemary Wray, copyeditor and proofreader David Abel, and publishers Richard Cohn and Cindy Black at Beyond Words Publishing; and to both of our families, who have contributed in so many ways to this creation.

Introduction

The real act of discovery is not in finding new lands,
but in seeing with new eyes.

— Marcel Proust

I HAVE TAKEN A FORTY-YEAR JOURNEY through the healing art of medicine, in search of what makes people sick and what makes them well. *Seeing Your Life Through New Eyes* is the result of that search. Donna and I invite you to explore a new way of seeing your life. The process that we present in this book, using techniques that we call Family Triangles and InSights, has been developed through years of use and refinement in counseling sessions, workshops, and personal work. It offers a roadmap to help you navigate to a new point of view—regarding your personal family history, your self-image, and the meaning of your life. True health is the acceptance and the appreciation of your life.

We look at how the gifts you received from your parents or significant caregivers in your childhood contributed to your understanding of love and to the values you cherish. We take an unconventional view of childhood hurts, and help you to see how they've shaped your life and relationships, in both healthy and unhealthy ways. We invite you to discover a new way of seeing your life—one that is realistic, creative, and gratifying.

Only by reenvisioning the events of childhood can we begin to free ourselves from the compulsion to repeat destructive patterns in our adult relationships. Only by seeing the gifts in the hurts of childhood can we come to the threshold of forgiveness—and even gratitude—for the painful, as well as the joyful experiences of life. When we rediscover the parts of ourselves that we've denied and embrace the parts of our life that we've rejected, we move back into the truth of our wholeness. This is true healing.

Often, the insights gained in counseling or therapy turn out to be short-lived, leaving nothing but vague memories of the steps that brought about a specific discovery. With Family Triangles, you will have a diagram for future reference—a map for understanding how your childhood experiences shaped your psychological and spiritual life journey. You will see clearly why you experience life the way that you do, and why you sometimes find yourself stuck in repeating patterns.

The Family Triangles process will help you understand how and whom you love, where and when you are limited by your assumptions and beliefs, and how you can move beyond old patterns and limiting ideas. You will begin to recognize your irrational expectations, and understand some of the reasons for your guilt, shame, and addictive behaviors. Most importantly, by moving through your Family Triangles, you will begin to see not only your unhealthy or hidden parts, but also your personal gifts and strengths.

The Family Triangles process will help make conscious what has been unconscious. This can help you to complete unfinished business while you're still healthy, instead of waiting until you're ill or even dying. Although this process focuses on your family of origin, and thus on your upbringing, it places no blame on your parents or caregivers, or on you, but rather invites you to look at life with greater clarity and forgiveness. This way of seeing helps you to embrace your life with more understanding, with gratitude, and with insights into new possibilities for healthy living and loving. It helps you to change misperceptions and misinterpretations of your life experiences, so you can begin to see your life through new eyes. You will start to see your most significant relationships as mirrors for self-reflection and healing. Emotional, physical, and spiritual health will blossom from a new appreciation and acceptance of your life as it was and as it is.

We don't see things as they are;
we see things as we are.
— Anaïs Nin

Family Triangles

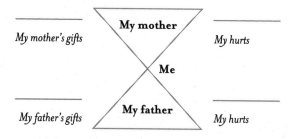

My mother's gifts   My hurts

My father's gifts   My hurts

Example

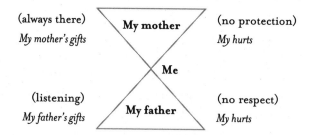

(always there)
My mother's gifts

(no protection)
My hurts

(listening)
My father's gifts

(no respect)
My hurts

One

Family Triangles

Don't turn your head.
Keep looking at the bandaged place.
That's where the light enters you.

— Rumi

As we enter a new millenium, there is a call for each of us to discover, own, and honor our unique gift to life. Our first tasks are to learn to meet our own unmet needs, to forgive and appreciate our past. This demands that we free ourselves of any attitudes or behavior patterns that interfere with our calling.

In reading this book and following its suggestions, you will have the opportunity to break through any nonproductive pattern that interferes with your relationships, career, health, or happiness. At the same time, you will be able to identify your own unique gift to life as well as learn effective skills for creative change. *Seeing Your Life Through New Eyes* presents the Family Triangles process and InSights, which offer you a way to free yourself from the limitations of the past by unravelling the illusions that keep you from living fully in the moment. In seeing your life through new eyes, with clear awareness, you'll see many signposts that point the way toward your life's purpose. *Seeing Your Life Through New Eyes* offers you a new beginning.

The original idea for the Family Triangles process came to Paul during a counseling session in the mid-1980s. Here's Paul's description of that session:

One day, a man entered my office hoping to resolve his issues around weight gain and unsuccessful relationships. He told me that whenever he was in one of his typically short-lived relationships, he tended to lose weight effortlessly. However, when he was alone, "the weight piled on."

As he spoke, I found myself doodling on a piece of paper; then, drawing a triangle, I asked him to talk about his parents.

He began: "My mother was extremely nurturing. She especially loved to feed me. But she was never really there for me emotionally."

"So there's a connection for you between food and nurturing?" I asked.

"I'm aware of that," he agreed. "I know that's how I feel nurtured. But why do I only need to stuff myself when I'm not in a relationship?"

"Perhaps it is a way of feeling nurtured when you're not in a relationship...?"

"That seems obvious, but what I don't understand then is why I can't seem to sustain a relationship!"

I wrote "nurturing" in one corner of a triangle and "emotionally not there" in the opposite corner; I wrote his name at the apex. It seemed clear to me that he had unconsciously created a kind of formula for his personal relationships. He had learned from his mother that nurturing not only equals food, but is also associated with someone who is not there emotionally. He watched me doodle, and then asked me what I was doing.

"Look at this," I said as I showed him the diagram. "'Nurturing,' for you, means eating. 'Emotionally not there' means no relationship. Your childhood programming might not allow room for a woman to be both 'there' emotionally and nurturing at the same time. Have you often felt that the women you're attracted to are not nurturing?"

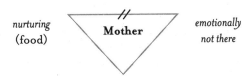

nurturing
(food)

Mother

emotionally
not there

Fascinated, he replied, "That's right!"

"So, from your mother you learned that nurturing, and eating, come with the experience of someone being absent, emotionally. Therefore, if someone is there emotionally, you unconsciously assume that nurturing is missing. It seems that you've mixed together the gift of nurturing

with the pain of a mother who was emotionally not there. It's hard to trust love
when that happens. And look here—"
I drew two lines at the top of the triangle
through the line between "nurturing" and
"emotionally not there." "On the one
hand, your mother nurtured you; on the
other hand, she was not there for you. This
seems like a mixed message that can lead to
even greater distrust of love relationships."

"Oh! So that's why I have trouble staying in an intimate relationship! And when
I'm not in a relationship, I gorge. Part of
me believes that nurturing cannot coexist
with someone being there. I really don't
trust love."

At this, he suddenly stood up, took the
piece of paper out of my hand, thanked
me enthusiastically, and left. The entire
session lasted no more than twenty minutes, but it started a process that would
continue to unfold for many years.

Donna, a Canadian therapist, was vis-
iting me at the time. When I told her
about the session, her response was: "It's
too simple!" However, later that day, we
played with the idea of using triangles to
look at our own parental gifts and hurts
from childhood.

We drew two triangles in an hourglass
configuration, with the mother's triangle
on top and the father's on the bottom. In
the center, where the points of the two tri-

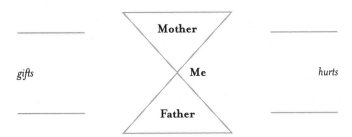

angles met, we wrote the word "me." On the left hand side, we wrote down the childhood "gifts" of our parents, and on the right hand side, our unmet needs as children (we labeled these the "hurts").

Within minutes, some of the key patterns in our lives became visually evident. The four words in the corners of those parental triangles all began to interact as a living process.

We were both aware of the childhood confusion that can result from unmet needs in childhood; this is well-known to psychotherapists. But it was astounding to realize how the patterns formed by the interplay of childhood gifts and hurts had been played out by our minds. The meanings we had made of these experiences as children had limited our lives as adults. As if released from the prisons of our own beliefs, we began to see—through the use of the Family Triangles—a new way of understanding these significant childhood experiences. This new way of seeing unfolded graphically as we drew it out on paper. We began to understand parts of ourselves we had never understood before.

The beauty and effectiveness of the Family Triangles process is that it is so graphic. It presents a picture of the journey we are on. In so doing, it gives us a kind of roadmap that shows us where we've come from and where we're headed. It helps us to see, not just conceptually, but graphically, the purpose and direction of our lives. We have used it successfully with people in all walks of life, in therapy sessions, in business settings, in workshops, with couples and families as well as individuals. Each person who has worked through their Family Triangles with us has helped the process to evolve. In this book, we have used many examples from our clients' experiences (changing the names to protect confidentiality). As you move through the following pages, you too may make discoveries about yourself that we could not have predicted.

The following suggestions are meant to help you as you move through the Family Triangles process. They are offered as helpful hints.

Hint 1. The kind of personal work we propose asks you to stretch beyond your old limits. Stretching properly does not mean forcing yourself to push through your limitations; it means acknowledging them, being willing to hang out at your edges, and letting them shift gradually. As with any kind of stretching, it is best to slow down, breathe, and pay attention to any resistance you may feel.

Hint 2. Find a quiet place and time in which to do this work. This can help you to remember such sensory memories as a smell, a taste, or images and colors associated with events from childhood. They may be emotional memories, perhaps overshadowed by anger. Notice that; acknowledge it.

Hint 3. You may wish to have a trusted friend, a close family member, or a supportive therapist with you as you move through this process; someone who can help you to make space for the experience that you're having, and to sort through old memories and assumptions as you look at yourself and your past in new ways.

Hint 4. Take your time, and move through the process with your feelings as well as with your mind. Pause frequently to check out what's happening in your body. Be calm, and open to your moment-to-moment experience.

Hint 5. Take a break between chapters to review your insights and options. Give yourself time to integrate each piece of the process before moving on to the next.

This is the use of memory:
For liberation—not less of love but expanding
Of love beyond desire, and so liberation
From the future as well as the past.
— T. S. Eliot

Two

Gifts

I have lived on the lip
of insanity, wanting to know reasons,
knocking on a door. It opens.
I've been knocking from the inside!

— Rumi

THE WAY YOU SEE YOUR OWN FAMILY OF ORIGIN may be affected by your unique genetic temperament as well as by your childhood experience. In studies of identical twins, genetic temperament has been shown to influence the choices made in life.[*] Your life journey began with your parents or primary caregivers, and your childhood experience of gifts, hurts, and disappointments: these became the very foundation of your ideas about love and pain. What do we mean to suggest by this?

"Gifts" are those things that you appreciated most about your parents. Your gifts may include qualities or attributes that you chose to acquire from a parent. Often, they are what you appreciated about a parent when you were between the ages of three and twelve. The gift may be a characteristic that you remember fondly, something

---

[*]James Kagen, "Temperament"; Robert Karen, *Becoming Attached*; Nancy Segal, *Entwined Lives*.

that your parent modeled. This was most likely a quality or characteristic or behavior that made you feel cared for and loved.

Let us show you how we use this idea of gifts to help people understand themselves and their relationships:

Sally was a woman of about thirty who came into the office tentatively, her blond curls half hiding her face. "How confidential is this?" she asked, the turn of her head further indicating mistrust and apprehension. "My employer wants me to come for therapy before I return to work, but I'm worried about how much you have to tell them."

After some reassurance about confidentiality, Sally talked about her situation. For several months, she'd been on stress leave from the law office where she worked. Sally was mostly concerned about going back because much of her stress was related to the other secretary, who she believed was constantly checking up on her. We learned that this was not the first work situation where trust issues with a coworker had caused her distress.

Sally was also struggling to let go of a relationship, even though it had been psychologically abusive. She said that people who knew her could not understand why she had stayed in it so long. She added that she had grown up with this kind of abuse, and so was surprised that she would put up with it again in an adult relationship.

We began to look at Sally's Family Triangles, explaining that our earliest relationships at home can program us for later problems, and that we might discover in her triangles some insights about what was happening now in her life. This would give her new ways to look at such situations, and some healthier possibilities for how she could respond. We looked at two very important aspects of Sally's childhood to see if we could find the roots of her issues there.

Sally thought about the gifts she had received from her parents; not what she could see now as an adult, but what had felt good to her as a child. Thinking first about her mother, Sally said, "she was always there." She described her as a traditional stay-at-home mom who took care of the family's needs. Sally felt certain of her mother's love as she grew up. It was much harder for Sally to come up with a gift from her alcoholic father. She remembered him as someone who was either absent, or verbally abusive when he came home drunk. As she thought about her childhood experience of her father, she finally remembered a time when her father had been kind to her, following a visit to her mother in the hospital. As she described what had happened, she recalled how he had showed an interest in her by paying attention and, most importantly, by listening.

The gifts from our parents become an important part of our definition of love. We learned to recognize love in that form, and we tend to show others love by offering the same gift or gifts. Usually, one of the parental gifts is especially significant. This cherished gift may come from the parent we felt most loved by; or, as in Sally's case, from an important, singular experience that was in contrast to an otherwise painful relationship.

Sally now recognized that she was being loved when someone paid attention to her and showed an interest by listening. However, because this gift of love was fused in childhood with the verbal abuse and disrespect she experienced from her father, she had come to repeatedly expect this same combination from life. She believed that if she wanted someone to pay attention to her, she could expect verbal abuse as well. When she recognized this expectation, Sally became intrigued, and began to see how it was a familiar pattern in her relationships.

Children tend to do two things above all with their childhood experiences: they take them personally, and they make them into general truths. A painful experience is almost always taken personally by a child: the young child often feels that he or she is the center of the universe. "I must be bad, unlovable, unworthy . . . this is about *me*." Events of childhood, especially in relationships with parents, later seem to be truths about reality: that's how a man behaves, that's what a marriage is like, that's how someone acts when they're angry, that's how someone shows love, and so on.

Sometimes the gifts come from people other than parents. Bob was a fiftyish businessman trying to change careers. He talked about his gifts:

The gift from my mother was creativity. I loved when she would play the piano. And she knitted the most beautiful sweaters in the world. I loved her hands. I appreciated her creativity. I can see that I got my creativity from her.

My father was killed in Vietnam when I was two years old, and so my grandfather was like a father to me. He took me fishing and taught me about nature. He was the kindest person I knew. The gifts from my grandfather are a love of nature, and kindness.

In one Family Triangles workshop, a woman ran into difficulty with the question about gifts. She was a dynamic red-haired artist whose flamboyant artwork expressed her vivacious personality.

Eve: *I'm stuck. For my mom, it's easy—strength and courage. But with my father, I can't get anything. He wasn't there, and all I can remember is my anger.*

Donna: *Why wasn't he there? Can you talk about him a little?*

Eve: *He was too busy being an entrepreneur—making money, losing money. He was always good to other people, but not to his own family.*

Donna: *There are some pretty special qualities that go into making an entrepreneur. I wonder if you see any of these qualities in yourself. Is there any part of you that's an entrepreneur?*

Eve (laughing): *Big deal! What if I am? Does that mean I am not available, like him?*

Donna: *We can look at that possibility later; first, let's find a gift if we can. In spite of the anger you have about him, perhaps* *being an 'entrepreneur' was a gift from your father—does that feel right?*

Eve: *Oh! I never saw him that way before—that's where it comes from. I am like my father that way! I never realized that before.*

YOUR GIFTS

Now let's walk through a process of identifying the gifts from your parents. (If stepparents, grandparents, aunts and uncles, or foster parents were your primary caregivers during your formative years, you might want to give separate answers for each of them; for now, choose your two primary caregivers, whom we'll refer to as mother and father.)

Try to let your answers come from a place of openness—what in Zen Buddhism is called a "beginner's mind." Even if your memory of a parent is primarily unpleasant, let your thoughts come from an open, beginner's mind. We're looking for something positive about your parents, even if it is sometimes hard to see at first.

Think about a time from your childhood, when you were between the ages of three and twelve.* Think about the house you lived in, your mother's room, where you had supper, where you felt safe. Try to recall or imagine your mother's face, the clothes she wore, how she smelled, how she felt, and how you felt loved.

---

*Jean Piaget, "The Growth of Logical Thinking."

In your mind's eye, let the years roll past. There's no need to analyze anything; just close your eyes, see the images, and feel whatever you feel. You may have a single memory of a brief moment with your mother, or repeated memories of something about her.

Take a quiet moment to reflect on your mother; then fill in the blanks.

My mother's gift to me was

_____

_____

Now take a look at your father's gift to you. Again, think about a time from your childhood, between the ages of three and twelve. Think about the house you lived in, your father's room, where you had supper, and where you felt safe, loved, or cared for by him. Avoid using the generalizations "love" or "survival." How did he demonstrate that he loved you?

Try to imagine your father's face, the clothes he wore, how he smelled, felt, and loved. Now try to recall what you appreciated the most about your dad. If more than one answer comes up, summarize these qualities into one or two gifts.

My father's gift to me was

_____

_____

Write these gifts on the Family Triangles Map in the Introduction.

What we appreciated most about our parents when we were children is what we now tend to emulate. What each of us chooses to emulate may also be influenced by our genetic temperament; nature and nurture combine to give us our gifts. Temperament might explain why siblings often discuss their childhoods as if they all had different sets of parents, and why each of them recalls different gifts! It could also explain why identical twins tend to see life through a similar lens and to choose similar experiences, even when they are separated at birth.*

---

*Stella Chess and Alexander Thomas, *Origins and Evolution of Behavior Disorders*; Segal, *Entwined Lives*.

Take a look at how your parental gifts define love.

I know I feel loved when

_____

_____

I know I am loving others when

_____

_____

How do these answers relate to my parental gifts?

_____

_____

Of the two gifts I received from my parents, the one that I cherish most is

_____

_____

Gifts

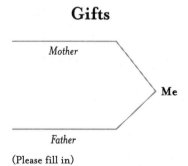

Mother

Me

Father

(Please fill in)

Notes

How We Love and Feel Loved

As we saw with Sally, people tend to be attracted to individuals who seem to offer gifts that are similar to those from parents.

Past relationships with others are retained within the mind and these residues shape the anticipation and often the actual perceptions of present and future relationships.
— Harry Stack Sullivan

This way of viewing present situations through the past can be conscious or unconscious, and is usually a combination of both. We tend to demonstrate our affection for others by offering them the same gifts that we appreciated from our parents. Our parents' gifts of love are now *our* gifts of love. They represent how we wish to be loved and how we show love to others.

Sally loved her children by being there for them, organizing her work schedule to be home when they got home from school and staying home evenings with them. And she listened to them when they told her about their day. Her gifts were "being there" and "listening."

The upside of your gifts from parents is that they now become the gifts that you have to offer to others. The downside is that if someone does not give you these same gifts, especially the one you cherish most, you might feel that they are not being loving. Your definition of love can therefore be very limited and static. Love from another person might be available, but you may be missing it if it is not the face of love that you have learned to recognize. The way your partner expresses love may not be your way.

Here's an example of such a situation: "I love my wife by offering her my most cherished parental gift of freedom, while what she actually seeks from me is the same closeness she received from her father. So when I give her space, she seems to interpret it as a lack of caring. And when she wants to demonstrate her love for me by being close, I feel suffocated."

The experience of love can get lost. It is offered, but not received as an expression of love. Neither person gets the love they're seeking. When any of us uses the word "love," we imagine that others share the same definition. Yet the aspects and qualities of love are infinite.

It's not unusual to take a perceived absence of love personally. "Why am I not lovable?" we may ask, "What is wrong with me?" We might blame ourselves as well as the other person. Since we were given a particular form of love in childhood, we often assume it to be our birthright. This sense of entitlement can give rise to irrational expectations and major disappointments.

BLAME

Blame is a typical reaction when we do not get what we feel entitled to—the gifts of love from our childhood. We tend to define love by one or both parental gifts, which means that if someone loves us, they are supposed to love us *that* way. We blame them for being unloving if they don't give us the same gifts of love that our parents gave us; Sally blamed her boyfriend more for his absence and not listening than for his abusiveness.

Here's an illustration from a Family Triangles workshop:

Husband: *What struck me was that my mother was always there. It was a gift of constancy. My father was so calm and peaceful. I cherished his peacefulness even more than her constancy.*

Wife: *That's funny. We have the same gift from our moms. She was always there for me. My father, like me, loved excitement. Between always being there for me and excitement, the gift I cherish most is excitement.*

Paul (to husband): *So, what happens when you're in your peaceful place, and she wants excitement?*

Husband: *Are you kidding? That's our battle. You nailed it! I can just hang out at home, but she's always looking for something to do. She can't sit still. She craves excitement.*

Wife: *I saw him the other night playing soccer. He scored this incredible goal and then walked away unemotionally—"Mr. Cool." It drives me crazy! I can't seem to decide whether to stay in the marriage or strike out for more excitement.*

Husband: *I never know if she is going to stay or leave. This creates excitement all right, but it is the bane of our existence. I don't feel I can trust our relationship.*

Paul: *Well, I'm curious about what happens when you are both living in your gifts of constancy?*

Husband and Wife (simultaneously): *That's heaven.*

Paul: *So the battleground is set when you're both caught up in your most cherished gifts: for him peacefulness, and for her excitement. It seems that when you're each in your father's gift, it's the War of the Roses! Then when you're both living in your mother's gifts—that is, constancy—it's "The Honeymooners"! We could say that your female psyches get along just great; it's the male parts that are in conflict.*

Recurring, drawn-out arguments in which neither partner is willing to budge usually occur because each partner has become entrenched in the need to have their most cherished gift. The arguments, then, are not between two adult partners, but between each person's inner child demanding the love (gift) of the parent!

Blame leads to anger over not getting a specific type of love. Our limited definitions of love often become the source of our unfulfilled expectations, blame, anger, and perhaps, in time, revenge. Paradoxically, when we consciously or unconsciously act out what we blame others for, this often leads to depression. Depression is anger turned inward.

Turning away from something ardently desired and loved cannot be unmixed with hate and revenge.
— Joan Riviere

Paralysis

We can go into a kind of paralysis when our parental gifts are paradoxical—that is, when they could not occur simultaneously without confusion or conflict. For example, if one parent's gift was play and the other parent's gift was a strong work ethic, you might feel paralyzed between wanting to play and needing to work. (Sally's gifts, always being there and listening, are not paradoxical in this way.)

The preceding example of the husband and wife demonstrates how our different definitions of love can paralyze us. The potential for the wife's paralysis was found in the discrepancy between her gifts of constancy and excitement. This paradox found its home in her thoughts: "Do I stay in this relationship or strike out for a more stimulating one?" She couldn't decide, and so felt stuck, and ambivalent about her marriage.

Her husband lived with uncertainty, too: "I never know if she's going to stay or leave. I don't trust the relationship." In addition to them blaming each other, she often blamed herself for her confusion. This was the source of her depression. Her husband, on the other hand, blamed himself for being the cause of her discontent. As a result, neither wife nor husband was fully available to themselves or to the relationship.

InSights

Look at how your parental gifts shape your experiences of love and blame.

I expect the person I love to

_____

_____

I blame them when

_____

_____

I blame myself when

_____

_____

Do my gifts seem contradictory or paradoxical?

_____

_____

If so, how do I feel stuck? What are my thoughts about that?

_____

_____

Am I angry because my mate has certain qualities that drive me crazy?

_____

_____

If so, I may tend to act out my anger by

_____

_____

How do the answers to these questions relate to my childhood gifts?

_____

_____

_____

Gifts

Mother

Me

Father

(Please fill in)

Notes

Values

The gifts from your parents affect not only how you love, and how you recognize love, but also what you value. Your most cherished values may stem directly from the gifts of your parents. These show up often in vocations and in corporate and business settings. Much dissatisfaction in the workplace stems from the discrepancy between employee values and management expectations.

Laura, a mid-forties single mother, worked in a corporate setting: "The gift I most appreciated from my mother was her pleasantness, her warmth; and I loved my father's intuitive abilities. Now I'm having difficulty at work; I find that management is cold. It seems that only productivity and left-brain mentality rule. I hate it!"

Rod was a physician: "The gift I most appreciated from my mother was her creativity, and from my father, his profound sense of loyalty. Since the private practice of medicine has been absorbed by managed care, there has been no opportunity to be creative. The system lacks inventiveness and compassion. The loyalty I felt toward my patients, and they toward me, has gone by the wayside. The values of managed care are in conflict with my own values. Now, going to work is a downer!"

In both of these examples, there's a conflict between management and employee values. The values and the environment of the workplace are as much the result of the CEO's childhood as the employee's values are the result of his or her childhood. Unfortunately, if neither party recognizes how these preferences shape and affect their lives, their attachment to their childhood gifts can cause problems and limitations.

With a new approach, Laura might be able to integrate intuition and intellect as a valuable new tool for productivity, and management could learn to use her intuition to its advantage. The physician who feels overpowered by managed care diminishes himself by not finding a way to maintain his own personal values while honoring the values of the organization. He's bitter toward "the system." The real work of healing is not in ridding ourselves of any of our parts, gifts, or childhood experiences, but in making space for other values and new ways of seeing.

In both business and personal settings, doing your Family Triangles can help you find ways to be more creative, innovative, and effective. This can be particularly helpful in areas where you feel stuck or blocked. Seeing through new eyes allows you to embrace what you have been rejecting or condemning. At the same time, it lets you relax your grip on whatever you've been clinging to, including your attachments to what you love and hate.

We are dominated by everything with which our self becomes identified. We can dominate and control everything from which we dis-identify ourselves.

— Robert Assagioli

The Shadow

The shadow hides what we think are our unlovable or unacceptable parts—what we don't want others to see. We tend to project these qualities onto others, blaming others for being "greedy," "selfish," "lazy," or "arrogant," rather than seeing any of these in ourselves. Hidden in your shadow are usually the opposites of your parental gifts, those qualities that are in direct conflict with your values.

For Sally, the shadow included the parts of herself that were not there for others or for herself, and her tendency not to listen, not to pay attention. Not being there for oneself is a kind of self-abandonment that can lead to various self-destructive behaviors. Sally could see that staying in an abusive relationship was a way of not being there for herself or her children. Until she could look at this shadow, she would continue to see herself as an innocent victim. The shadow element of your self-image may hide your personal power. It can also lead to unfair comparisons, judgements, and criticisms, both of yourself and others.

In spite of Rod's need for creativity and loyalty, he began to admit that he, too, tended to avoid certain responsibilities. Rather than seeing his own feelings of disloyalty and lack of care, he had displaced these shadow qualities onto managed care and judged that the system was uncaring.

Laura, who "hated work," projected coldness onto management, without acknowledging her own similar feelings towards work. There were times when she, like anyone, was unpleasant. And she, too, used her intellect as much as her intuition. Yet, these were qualities that she would rather not see in herself. Instead, she complained about the workplace being too intellectual and cold.

Laura's and Rod's thoughts, desires, and actions were sometimes contrary to their values from childhood gifts. And when they recognized this about themselves, they felt depressed and ashamed. When this happened, they immediately put the lid on their feelings and directed their anger, their unfaced shadow, toward the situation at work. The discrepancy between the gift (what they loved and valued about themselves) and the hidden opposite became their shame, anger, and source of depression. Others can see this too and may call it hypocrisy.

Distrust is a natural result of the mixed messages between the gifts we act out and the shadow qualities we try to hide. Let's look at how a gift may hide a shadow quality that impacts relationships. There are many other aspects to the shadow, which we'll explore later. To understand this part of the shadow, look at the opposites of gifts and how they play out in relationships. We have seen how the opposites of Sally's gifts turned into a kind of self-abandonment—where she was not there for herself.

Here's an example from a Family Triangles workshop:

Husband: *My mother's gifts were freedom and compassion. From my father, the gifts were an interest in so many things, and* his way of sharing skills. This fits with how I love and how I recognize love, and with my profession as a therapist. I love sharing with my wife, but there are times I feel smothered.

Donna (turning to wife): What were your gifts?

Wife: From my father it was protection, and from my mother, joy.

Donna: Let's look at how your triangles fit together here. One of your gifts was protection. Can you see how that might affect your husband?

Wife: Well, I think he feels his freedom is limited at times when I'm just trying to protect him . . . or when I need him to protect me.

Husband: Right . . . at times, I feel stifled because she's overly concerned about what will happen to me, the kids, and to herself. I can feel her dependency. At the same time, she often complains about taking care of others and never having time for herself. All this gets in the way of our relationship.

Wife: I don't know why I worry about him and the kids so much. I don't know what he is talking about . . . I can take care of myself and I am not resentful about taking care of others.

Donna: Let's continue. Your cherished gift of freedom has a shadow side—as do all our gifts. What is the opposite of freedom for you?

Husband: That would be dependency. I hate to feel dependent!

Donna: Just sit with that for a moment . . . when you consider the idea of being dependent, what happens for you?

Husband (after a moment): It's so hard! I feel like I'm trapped . . . suffocated. It's definitely about loss of freedom. My whole body gets anxious.

Donna: It's great that you're in touch with that now. So, rather than admitting your dependency, because it feels so much as if you'll lose your freedom, you might unconsciously invite your wife to limit your freedom, which she does through her need to

protect you and to be protected. Your dependency gets projected onto her. You might have actually unconsciously hired her to play the smothering wife!
Wife: *I'd like a new job description please! (laughter)*

It's not uncommon to choose a mate who acts out our shadow. We might be drawn to someone as an unconscious drive for self-repair and balance. Rather than accepting all our disowned parts, we blame our mates for limiting us when they may actually be offering us the potential for healing. Relationship is a form of mirror therapy.

Donna *(to wife):* *Let's turn to the gift—protection—and look at the shadow side. What's the opposite?*
Wife: *Hmmm . . . maybe . . . being unprotected . . . ?*
Donna: *And what does it mean to be unprotected? Just sit with it for a moment and feel the answer that comes up.*
Wife: *. . . well . . . exposed! It feels very vulnerable.*
Donna: *I can see that it's very uncomfortable for you to feel that vulnerability, isn't it? Does it bring up any impulses?*
Wife: *I can feel a part of me that wants to turn my attention to him . . . take care of him!*
Donna: *So you may project your vulnerability onto him and feel yourself wanting to protect him. That may feel better than sitting in the uncertainty of your own vulnerability.*
Wife: *Oh my God, that's so true. I can feel right now how much I hate the "what if" feeling that goes with being vulnerable.*

When we are willing to live in uncertainty, it can move us toward unlimited opportunity. This woman now has more choice. Holding on to protectiveness rather than being willing to experience vulnerability was not only limiting her choices, but was dishonest, as was her husband's holding on to freedom while actually feeling dependent. Both of their shadow parts—dependency and vulnerability—are essential for intimacy. What they both were in search of was to be found within their disowned shadow parts.

It's as if both partners were vicariously living through each other. This can eventually lead to resentment or jealousy, since one mate is acting out what the other is unwilling to accept in themself.

Wife: *So, when we are blaming each other, it's really our shadow parts speaking!*
Donna: *Right! Our shadow parts, those hidden, unconscious parts of ourselves that we usually project onto others, can lead to blame, shame, finger pointing, resentment, and jealousy.* *
Husband: *So does this mean I'm supposed to become dependent? That doesn't feel so good.*
Donna: *The way to bring our shadow parts into the light is to begin to see some beauty in these qualities . . . (turning to wife) What's the beauty of being vulnerable?*
Wife: *. . . well . . . I feel more open . . . sensitive . . . I know it feels better whenever I let myself be vulnerable with my friends and they offer comfort and tenderness.*
Donna *(to husband):* *Is there a beauty or gift in being dependent? Can you get beyond your aversion to it and see another possibility?*
Husband: *Well . . . I can see that it could lead to more intimacy. I know that's what she wants. The truth is, I am dependent on her*

---

*Carl Jung, *The Undiscovered Self.*

and on the relationship, for a lot of things. My real fear is, what if I'm dependent and no one shows up?

Donna: *That is scary. How can you be OK with living in that uncertainty?*

Husband: *By seeing it now for what it is. By just admitting it, I'm getting more comfortable with it. That helps. And . . . by feeling the excitement . . . the new possibilities that open up . . . that feels good!*

In general, we aren't likely to choose someone for a love relationship who doesn't offer us our cherished gift; we may, however, be unconsciously attracted to a reflection of our own shadow. By the time a relationship becomes "chronic" (which means that the honeymoon is over), our shadow parts start to emerge, first as projections. If my gift is excitement, I might blame others for being boring, yet actually be ashamed of my own dullness.

I may project boredom (which is the shadow side of excitement) onto my partner because I don't want to acknowledge it in myself. The beauty or gift hidden in boredom is peace. When we can acknowledge our shadow and bring it into balance with our parental gifts, it becomes a gift in itself, a part of our authentic self.

To be 'authentic' is to be true to oneself, to be what one is, to be 'genuine.' To be 'inauthentic' is to not be oneself, to be false to oneself: to be not as one appears to be, to be counterfeit.
— R. D. Laing

We are living from our *authentic self* when our inner thoughts and feelings match our outer behaviors. This demands that we take back all our projections and disowned parts. We are authentic when we live in trust, accepting life as it is, with all its uncertainty.

Until you can look appreciatively at all your hidden parts, you haven't faced your greatest fear—your own shadow. Yet your shadow holds within it the treasures that you seek. Ignoring these parts keeps you from remembering your wholeness. Sally was eventually able to see that when someone was not there for her, not paying attention, she had a certain freedom. Freedom is the gift in abandonment. She discovered that she could be there for herself and others at times, and at other times, be free.

Psychotherapists work to get parts communicating, whether it is members of a family, the body and the mind or parts of mind. . . . This process of communication organizes parts into wholes. That's the healing.

— Ron Kurtz

InSights

Consider the ways your parental gifts influence you in your relationships.

I admire and value people who demonstrate my parental gifts of

_____

_____

I can't tolerate it when people demonstrate the opposites of those gifts:

_____

_____

When I argue with my partner, lover, friend, or coworker, I know I am right when they act out the opposites of my gifts:

_____

_____

When I argue with my partner, lover, friend, or coworker, I know I am wrong when I do things I can't seem to control, like

_____

_____

I trust people who

_____

_____

I distrust people who

_____

_____

People trust me when I

_____

_____

People distrust me when I

_____

_____

*How are the answers to these questions related to the gifts of
my childhood?*

_____

_____

What are the opposites of my gifts?

_____

_____

*How could these opposite traits and gifts possibly benefit
my life?*

_____

_____

Notes

Theory has worth as preparation only;
the critical struggle lies in the Act.

— Nikos Kazantzakis

Summary

No observer of human behavior can fail to
notice that people act on the basis of the
meaning which they attribute to their experience
of themselves and of the world around them.

—Jay Greenberg and Stephen Mitchell

Your life journey began with your parents, the foundation of your love and pain, of your gifts and hurts. Throughout life, your actions are based upon how you understood these earliest relationships. Your childhood interpretation of the world around you has become a belief system that shapes your adult relationships and your identity. Over time, your reality may have become a self-fulfilling prophecy.

We carry our parents or significant caregivers inside us for a very long time. We incorporate them into almost every thought and action. What we appreciated most in childhood shapes how we love and what we value. As we have seen, these childhood gifts can also create limitations. In time, our childhood gifts can lead to our adult addictions.

By widening your perspective, you begin to see your life through new eyes. Once you have explored the shadows (opposites) of your cherished gifts, you'll find that they are as valuable to you as the gifts themselves. The gift has a shadow; the shadow hides a gift. As your personal values begin to open to and embrace the values of others, love takes on a greater dimension and more possibilities.

Many of us are living lives similar to those of our parents—never realizing the truth of our own specialness. We need to take back our disowned parts if we are ever to discover our unique beauty. There is a wonderful maxim in the Kabala that says that when you meet someone who tells you your story, you meet your soul. The people we meet in our lives are often the healing mirrors of our souls. To honor them is to honor ourselves. To honor all relationships is a spiritual path.

There is no need for blame. When we find the beauty in what we once rejected, forgiveness occurs effortlessly. If we turn away from our imagined ugliness, we are simultaneously turning away from our own beauty.

Why do you stay in prison
when the door is so wide open?

— Rumi

Three

Hurts

*Whoever finds love
beneath hurt and grief*

*disappears into emptiness
with a thousand new disguises.*

— Rumi

WHEN WE SPEAK OF "HURTS," we mean unmet childhood needs. The hurt refers to what you wanted but felt you didn't receive from your parents. It might be something your parent did or didn't do that made you feel unsafe, unloved, or unlovable. Hurts can make you question your worthiness or make you feel insecure.

As children, we did not have the awareness to say, "I need my father's (or mother's) acceptance." Yet, we were affected by his or her nonacceptance. In what way were you impacted, emotionally, by something your parents did or did not do?

A hurt may range from an uncomfortable or painful experience to a traumatic one, or consist of repeated childhood experiences in relation to your parent or caregiver, especially when you were between the ages of three and twelve. The hurt was a need unmet—something you wanted from your parents but felt you did not receive.

Sally looked at the hurts from her parents.

My father was so mean to me . . . verbally abusive. I needed him to be more respectful of me. The hurt was not getting respect. Mom was always there, but she didn't protect me from him. She had no backbone to stand up to him. What I needed from her but didn't get was protection.

You may have difficulty recalling any parental hurt. Many people find it impossible to think of their parents negatively: "I cannot think of a single thing my mom ever did to hurt me. She was the best!" There may have been no apparent or intentional hurt, but it's unlikely that every childhood need was met. All children feel hurt from time to time, even with the best of parents.

Even the absence of any hurt from a parent can be an unmet need. It is not uncommon for a child to be absorbed into a parent's identity. Although this may initially offer the child a sense of security, it can obscure the sense of a separate self. The child's journey through life may be parent-centered rather than ego-centered, where every thought and action is directed by the wishes of the parent (or internalized parent) and not by the person's own authentic needs. Separate ego development—"individuation"—is a vital component of a fully functional person. A childhood hurt can serve as the cutting of the emotional umbilical cord to allow for healthy ego development.

Even if every memory of your parent/caregiver seems wonderful, try to let your thoughts come from your beginner's mind. You can usually recall at least one hurtful experience. As an adult, you may look at your past with more understanding and be able to understand or justify an unmet need. For now, put this adult perspective aside and see again through the eyes of the child you were. When a hurt stays unconscious, it can have a stronger effect on your life and relationships than when it is remembered.

Even a single hurtful experience can make an impression that lasts. Jeremy had a hard time coming up with a hurt from his mother. Then he remembered something:

> My dad worked a lot. He was hardly ever home. But my mom was always there for me. One day, when I was seven, my dad came home early from work and told my mom he was taking her out to dinner. I asked if I could tag along. My mom said no. That is the only negative experience with my mom that I can remember—the only time she ever let me down. Even though this happened only one time that I can recall in my childhood, I never forgot it. The hurt was that I felt she left me out. Even though I was only seven, I do remember how I tried to figure out what it was about me that made her not want to have me with her.

Think about your own childhood between the ages of three and twelve. Think again about the house you lived in and your room. What did you do and where did you go when you felt hurt? What situation or event comes to mind that created this hurt?

Can you recall something your mother did that upset you, or something you wanted from her, but didn't receive? This memory could be related to the way she treated you or a way in which she neglected you. Don't simply answer, "She did not love me"—describe specifically how she failed to show her love for you. What did you need from your mother that you felt you did not get? If there was more than one hurt, which one or two come up right now as significant?

Again, please take the time to sit quietly, and to feel the questions in your body as well as notice the emotional quality and validity of your responses. Notice what sensations are evoked, along with the memories and images. Pay attention to the feeling quality of your experience.

However even if you were fortunate enough to grow up in a safe, nurturing environment, you still bear invisible scars from childhood, because from the very moment you were born you were a complex, dependent creature with a never-ending cycle of needs. Freud correctly labeled us "insatiable beings." And no parents, no matter how devoted, are able to respond perfectly to all of these changing needs.
— Harville Hendrix

If you are still stumped about a possible hurt, consult the list of suggestions in the Appendix (page 153). In order to get the most out of this process, spend some time soul-searching before referring to the list.

We are wounded simply by participating in human life, by being children of Adam and Eve. To think that the proper or natural state is to be without wounds is an illusion. Any medicine motivated by the fantasy of doing away with woundedness is trying to avoid the human condition.

—Thomas Moore

Take a quiet moment now to recall your mother when you were a child between the ages three and twelve, then fill in the blanks:

The hurt from my mother was

_____

_____

Now use the same process for your father.

The hurt from my father was

_____

_____

Write your hurts on the Family Triangles Map in the Introduction.

PEOPLE SKILLS

Pain is indelibly imprinted in our memory. Not only do we attempt to avoid a repetition of painful memories, most of us also try hard not to subject others to similar experiences.

Remembering our childhood pain gives us a chance to find within it a hidden gift. The opposites of our hurts can be the sources of some of our *people skills*. Because we do not want to do something to someone else that was painful for us, we tend to do for others the very opposite of our childhood hurts or unmet needs.

Thus, by reversing a situation, namely in acting towards another person as a good parent, in phantasy we re-create and enjoy the wished-for love and goodness of our parents.
— Melanie Klein

Melissa, a young social worker in one of our workshops, spoke sadly about herself:

My father was abusively critical. I never got anything right. My mother just wasn't there for me . . . I see now that I needed my dad to accept me and for my mom to be there when I needed her. These are my people skills: I am very accepting of other people, and I'm really there for others— I'll always put myself out for others. On the other hand, if a situation arises where I am either critical of someone, or not there when they need me, I feel huge pangs of guilt.

GUILT

You are likely to feel guilty when you see yourself inflicting upon someone else the same hurt that you experienced as a child. We are differentiating here between guilt and shame. As John Bradshaw has pointed out, guilt is about something we have or have not *done*; shame, on the other hand, has to do with feeling bad about who we *are*. Guilt, he points out, says "I did something wrong," while shame says "There's something wrong with me."*

Jeremy, who had difficulty finding a hurt from his mother other than a unique experience of being left behind, later found himself feeling guilty when he left another person out of any situation. In fact, a bone of contention between him and his wife was that he always invited other people to "tag along" in their lives. In her words, "Jeremy is someone who collects 'stray dogs' everywhere we go." The opposite of his hurt was his need to include others. He felt guilty if he left someone out. Though Jeremy was

---

*John Bradshaw, *Healing the Shame that Binds You*.

unable to find more than this one hurt, we see how even one isolated painful incident can shape adult behavior.

Your people skills can emerge out of the pain of your childhood unmet needs. We try to give to others what we felt we needed but did not get from our parents. When we are unable to do this we often feel guilty. This kind of guilt is part of our conscience, and can become a pathway to empathy and compassion.

In the depths of the mind, the urge to make people happy is linked up with the strong feeling of responsibility and concern for them, which manifests itself in genuine sympathy with other people and in the ability to understand them as they are and as they feel. . . . we can put ourselves in the place of other people.
— Melanie Klein

Here's an example from a Family Triangles workshop:

Lydia: *From my mother, the hurt was lack of support, lack of protection. And from my father, it's that he never took responsibility for his feelings. He always blamed everybody else.*
Paul: *So, what you needed from your mother was support and protection, and what you needed from your father was for him to be responsible and accepting. Are those some of your people skills?*

Lydia: *This says so much about me! I mean, I can see this with my husband, and with my children and how I'm raising them, and how I'm trying so much to balance it all. I'm trying to find the place now where I can just relax, you know? I get that it's about me. I've been down the road with putting it on them, and now I'm at a place where I realize that it's about me.*

Paul: *It sounds like you're accepting all the responsibility and you seem to be exhausted from your need to support and protect others.*

Lydia: *I can see how I support, protect, and accept my friends, and even feel responsible for them. I feel responsible for everybody's feelings. When one of my friends is down, I even feel guilty, as if. . . you know . . . I caused it. The truth is, though, that I'm far more supportive, protective, and accepting of my friends than of my kids or husband.*

Paul: *This often tends to be the case. We call the long-term live-in relationships, where we re-create our childhood hurts, "chronic relationships." Living together tends to call up our childhood family situation and triggers these old programs and patterns differently from friendships and short-term, casual relationships. We'll look at this again later.*

InSights

Think about the ways in which your childhood hurts and unmet needs affect you now.

The opposites of my hurts are

_____

_____

These are my people skills.

I feel guilty when I am not able to

_____

_____

How do I use my people skills in work? In personal relation-ships?

_____

_____

Hurts

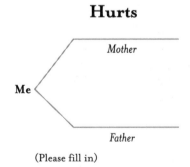

(Please fill in)

Notes

VOCATION

Our people skills usually prove to be important in our chosen vocation, and are often involved in our choice of work and career. The pain we experienced in childhood can help our souls and psyches to grow, and may direct us to serve others in specific ways, as we'll see in the following examples.

Ben: *The hurts from my father were lack of connection and lack of physical contact. It seemed impossible to get any physical affection from him.*
Paul: *What kind of work do you do?*
Ben: *I do bodywork and massage.*
Paul: *That's amazing! And what did you need from your mom that you didn't feel you got?*
Ben: *Validation . . . empowerment.*
Paul: *And can you tell us how that fits with the way you do bodywork?*
Ben: *Well . . . I'm constantly empowering my clients to be in touch with themselves and to get what they need in our sessions by participating actively.*

(Another participant spoke up at this point.)
Sarah: *I have some sorting out to do here. I thought for the longest time that my unmet need for intellectual stimulation was connected to my mother. But that was really the hurt from my dad. What I didn't learn from my mother was how to have fun.*
Paul: *Often we do for others what wasn't done for us. Does intellectual stimulation and fun figure significantly in your life now?*

Sarah: *Sure, in my work with Alzheimer's patients. I connect with these people instinctually through stimulating them with play.*

Paul: *That's great! You needed intellectual stimulation and fun as a child, and now that's what you give to the people you work with.*

(Another participant asked a question.)

Carol: *What happens if you hate what you're doing?*

Paul: *"Hate" is a strong word. Well, let's look at that—and why you're stuck there.*

Carol: *Did you have to use the word "stuck"? (laughter)*

Paul: *Tell us the gifts and hurts from your parents.*

Carol: *The gift from my mother was freedom, and the gift from my father was his drive, his persistence. My mother was not there for me, while my father was critical.*

Paul: *Your mother's gift of freedom and your father's gift of drive seem somewhat paradoxical—and this can be confusing. Freedom is having a sense of choice, whereas drive tends to push us relentlessly. This confusion might lead to the paralysis of not knowing whether to make yourself stay in a job or leave.*

Carol: *That's true!*

Paul: *At the same time, your hurts—not being there and criticism—are also paradoxical. This can lead to a sense of victimization. You may feel hurt either way. Your mother was not there; while your father, by being critical, was—pardon the expression—in your face. How does this relate to your confusion about whether to stay in the job or leave?*

Carol: *That about sums it up. The job heightens an old familiar feeling of being trapped. Sometimes I want to jump out of my skin.*

Paul: *Your body may bear the brunt of the confusion you feel emotionally. If you let your body tell you more about this feeling* *and about what it needs, you might be able to feel what to do with it.*

Carol: *If I don't resist the feeling, I can sense that my body wants to move . . . When I let myself move, I feel calmer inside. Wow! It's not the job, as much as a need for movement at all levels—mind, body, spirit.*

InSights

Think about the connections between your work life and your personal life.

My people skills (opposites of hurts) serve me at work by

_____

_____

_____

My people skills do not serve me at work because

_____

_____

_____

Where I sometimes feel stuck is

_____

_____

_____

The Real Pain of Childhood Hurts

Our people skills are often most evident in our non-intimate relationships—at work, in play, in friendship. However, in long-term, intimate, live-in relationships, which become chronic relationships, we tend to inflict on our mates the same hurts that we experienced as children. We stress "long-term" and "live-in" because this is when the home environment recalls our family of origin and evokes similar feelings and reactions. It is here that we tend to relate to family members in the same way that we were parented. Or we may see our mates as we saw our parents, not seeing them as the unique beings they are.

Recall Lydia, the woman who was so accepting and present for her friends and coworkers, but found herself far more critical and far less available for her husband and children. Her husband wondered, "Why can't you be the same lovable person with me as you are with the rest of the world?"

Jeremy, who had all those "stray dog" friends, periodically isolated himself when he was at home. In his words, "I love being with my family, but sometimes I just need my solitude." His wife complained, "He's available for the rest of the world, but when I need him he's never available."

Projection is the mechanism by which we deny responsibility for and externalize a thought or feeling . . . by holding someone else responsible for it.
— Gerald Jampolsky

Since our original hurts are so familiar, we may unconsciously seek them out. In fact, we might misinterpret any painful experiences as repetitions of the original childhood hurts.

Lynn felt that the pain from her father in childhood was his anger. When her husband was critical of her behavior, she interpreted his comments as anger. He responded, "I'm not angry. I'm just being critical." In turn, when she was angry at her husband—as her father had been with her—her husband felt criticized. She responded, "I'm not being critical. I'm just pissed off."

In these moments, the adult parts of both the husband and wife checked out while their child parts went to battle. This is a game of emotional volleyball, but in this case it's as if the players are each spiking the ball into their own court.

It looks to me as if all of us must make our peace with these mean impulses within ourselves. And my impression so far is that the best way to do this is to transmute envy, jealousy, presentiment, and nastiness into humble admiration, gratitude, appreciation, adoration, and even worship via conscious insight and working through.

— Abraham Maslow

InSights

Look at how the hurts from your childhood and
their opposites (your people skills) affect your
adult relationships.

(People skills) With my friends, I'm usually

_____

_____

_____

(Hurts) In long-term, intimate relationships, I tend to be

_____

_____

_____

When I disagree with my mate, it feels similar to being

   with my mother   *with my father*   *with both*

(please circle one)

How do my answers to these questions reflect my childhood hurts?

_____

_____

_____

Internalized Parents

As a very young child, you had few boundaries to differentiate yourself from your surroundings. You imagined that you were the center of your universe, and that you were responsible for the problems around you. As adults, we all may carry within us a lingering echo of that very young child, at times feeling responsible for things beyond our control.

Perhaps the greatest abuse that comes from our family of origin is the self-abuse we suffer when we continue to parent ourselves the way we were originally parented. Our unconscious critic may be our *internalized parent*, and it can drive us incessantly.* This is the voice of self-deprecation—the voice that reminds us of our unworthiness, telling us, "You're not enough! Do more! Do more! Be more! Be more!"

By adulthood, we may not accept love, because a part of us doesn't trust it. We don't trust love when we feel unworthy of it. Nor did we trust our parents' love. "How can they both love me and hurt me?" Love seemed doubtful and mixed with pain. This is why love can hurt. A child has a tendency to interpret the hurt to mean, "there must be something wrong with me." Over time, this idea can become a personal truth.

Children, living in the paradox, "How can my parents both love and hurt me?" may confuse the gift of love with the pain or unmet need, thus

---

*Melanie Klein, *Psychoanalysis of Children*.

creating an internal conflict. This fusion of love with pain, and the resulting confusion we feel, creates distrust of love. We felt betrayed by love; our history taught us that love comes with pain.

As children, we also felt betrayed if one parent did not protect us from the other. Now, as adults, we may betray ourselves in an identical manner by not protecting ourselves. Sally is an example of someone who continued as an adult to subject herself to abusive relationships. She assumed that to feel loved and have someone's attention meant inevitably that she would be verbally abused and treated with disrespect. When she was a child, her mother did not stand up for her against the abuse of her father. As an adult, she could not stand up for herself against the abuse of her boyfriends.

The internalized critical parent can continue to give us the same negative messages we heard or imagined as children. If this stays unconscious, it can create barriers to intimacy. "If someone gets too close, they'll find out how unworthy (stupid, useless, lazy, ugly, crazy) I really am."

The internalized parent is like a shotgun we put to our heads. Seeking love from another from the place of no self-love only temporarily fills the void. Parenting ourselves the way we were parented can be a humiliating form of self-punishment, and shame—a black hole in which even the love of another is never truly appreciated or received.

Why do we allow these negative patterns to run our lives?

As much as we cherish the gifts of love from our parents, we are as dearly attached to the hurts! Because the two appeared to go together, we're afraid that to let go of one (the hurt), we would need to give up the other (the gift). Or we may hold onto the idea of being hurt so as not to forgive the parent. To forgive a parent, or other primary caregiver, might be very difficult. True forgiveness means letting go of the hurt that also binds us to their love. The hurt clings to the love and the love clings to the hurt. The first step in letting go is seeing the two experiences as separate events, not necessarily inevitably linked together in life.

The Gift in the Hurt

There is often another unconscious reason for our attachment to a childhood hurt. A hurt can seem to legitimize a behavior from which we benefit. If, for example, as a child, you could not count on one or both of your parents to be there, that may have given you a certain freedom; and you may now use that same freedom to do things your own way. You may have become extremely attached to freedom. Your sense of freedom can become linked to the idea that you couldn't count on your parents, or more generally, that you can't count on anyone. You might fear losing your freedom if you give up that idea.

Such benefits (like freedom) are not the same as coping skills, which we will discuss later. Your coping skills are the talents and strategies that you perfected to protect yourself from feeling your childhood pain, or to try to get your needs met. Here, we are referring to the hidden gifts that emerge from your experiences of childhood hurts or unmet needs. This recognition does not in any way justify inappropriate parental behavior, but it allows you to appreciate the fact that you can turn your hurts into something of value.

It is not automatic, however. Freedom, for example, can become an unconscious addiction. In spite of saying, "I want someone to be there for me" or "I crave intimacy in my life," a hidden gift of freedom (the result of unavailable parents) can unconsciously motivate you to sabotage relationships. There is almost always a gift hidden in an unmet need; it may be freedom or attention. The hidden gift does not diminish the pain of the unmet need; the question is how to meet the unmet need without losing the gift.

To understand yourself more fully, you have to look at every facet of your life and see the choices you've made that have shaped who you are today. In this way, you can better understand how you influence your own reality. You can learn to see that you have more choice about changing anything that interferes with living a life that is fully functional—what Carl Rogers called "the good life."*

Here's an example of finding a gift hidden in the hurt:

---

*Carl Rogers, *On Becoming a Person*.

Pamela: *I don't see any benefit in not having been seen by my mother.*

Pamela's friend: *Something that occurs to me in knowing you is that one of the gifts of not having been seen might be your transparency. You have chameleonlike qualities. You move in and out of situations better than anyone else I know. You never stand out as a jarring part of any situation.*

Pamela: *Uh-huh. Thanks. I know that; I like my chameleon-like abilities. But why can't I just stand out sometimes and be seen for who I am?*

Donna: *Isn't it interesting how rapidly you discounted your friend's analysis of you? It was "Thanks, but . . ." Would there be any reason to enjoy being the chameleon more than standing out and being seen? Notice what happens as she tells you again that you move in and out of situations better than anyone she knows.*

(Pamela listened as her friend repeated the compliment.)

Pamela: *It's hard to let it all in. I'm aware of not wanting too much attention focused on me . . . as if even more might be expected of me if I'm noticed. There's a part of me that would rather go unnoticed . . . thanks! Even doing this process now in the group is making me nervous.*

Paul: *We're often looking for someone to meet our unmet needs, but we are usually afraid of losing the gift hidden in the hurt. The gift of being unnoticed and therefore not seen is what?*

Pamela: *Well, it gives me a certain amount of freedom. But I'd still like to be seen . . . sometimes?*

Paul: *Nothing wrong with that! If you were suddenly faced with having the choice between being seen or having freedom, which would you choose?*

Pamela *(without hesitation)*: *Freedom!*

Paul: *How can you have it all—freedom and being seen?*

Pamela: *Hmmm . . . by seeing and acknowledging myself. That's neat!*

How have you become attached to the unconscious benefits of your unmet needs? (This can not only get in the way of meeting the needs you are in search of, but can become destructive and, ultimately, addictive.)

My most common negative thoughts about myself are

_____

_____

_____

I criticize myself most when

_____

_____

_____

I feel unloved when

_____

_____

_____

When I am feeling unloved, I blame

_____

_____

_____

I hide my feelings by

_____

_____

_____

I don't trust love because

_____

_____

_____

I feel betrayed when

_____

_____

_____

I fear intimacy because

_____

_____

_____

If someone gets too close, I fear they will discover

_____

_____

_____

I prevent intimacy by

_____

_____

_____

The gift in the hurt is rarely recognized; but it is a major obstacle to intimacy. Like the cherished gift, the gift hidden within the hurt can become addictive.

The gift in my hurt is

_____

_____

_____

The benefit of the unmet need prevents me from

_____

_____

_____

How can I get my unmet needs met without losing the hidden gift found within the hurt?

_____

_____

_____

How do my answers to these questions reflect my parental hurts?

Where in my body do I feel the answers, or the fear of them?

Hurts

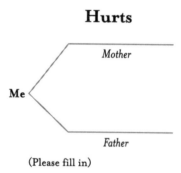

Me

Mother

Father

(Please fill in)

VICTIMIZATION

Let's look at your parental hurts. Are they paradoxical? Does one seem to contradict the other? If your answer is "yes," you will soon understand why you might sometimes feel victimized. For example, one of your hurts could be suffocation, while the other parent's hurt was that they were never there. Then, in an intimate relationship, when your partner tries to be close, you may tend to feel that he or she is suffocating you. And when they are not there, you may tend to feel abandoned. Relationship may seem to offer you no safe place to stand. It can seem like a no-win situation!

The truth is that there is a happy medium. A good relationship is a dance between aloneness and togetherness, between separation and union. This dance demands that you find comfort in aloneness and in uncertainty. Accepting aloneness can lead to security, while accepting uncertainty leads to freedom.

Living with the paradox of security and freedom can open the gateway to living more passionately and intimately.

Maturity, or self-actualization, from this point of view, means to transcend the deficiency-needs.
— Abraham Maslow

And, speaking of the adult as well as the child,

He must learn to gratify his own needs and
wishes, rather than the needs of his parents,
and he must learn to gratify them himself . . .
He must give up being good out of fear and in
order to keep their love, and must be good
because he wishes to be. He must discover his
own conscience and give up his internalized
parents as a sole ethical guide.

— Abraham Maslow

HEALING OUR UNMET NEEDS

We all have the skills to heal the emotional pain and the unmet needs of our childhoods. Healing takes place when we can be as good to ourselves as we are to our friends. Look at the opposites of your hurts—your people skills—and jot down all the qualities that go into expressing those skills. When you are with a friend in need, and that need is similar to the hurt of your childhood, what do you do? How do you do it? Try to take a moment to tap into what you do to meet the needs of a friend.

Shirley: *The hurts of my childhood were that I was not accepted by my father, and that my mother was not there. When any of my friends are having problems, I'm the first to be there for them and am completely accepting of their situation and their needs.*
Paul: *How do you do this with your friends? How do you demonstrate that you're there and accepting?*
Shirley (*after thinking for a moment*): *For acceptance, I listen, I'm present, I'm open, I'm not judgmental, I try to feel where*

they're at. To be there for others, I'm quick to respond, I'm available for whatever need might arise, I'm concerned, and I follow up. I also listen intently, silently. I try to feel what is happening. I am really there.

Paul: *These are keys to learning how to meet these needs for yourself. When was the last time you listened to yourself, were present and open to yourself, as well as not being judgmental?*

Shirley: *It's been awhile—maybe never. It sure feels easier to do it for others.*

Paul: *When we're down, it's so hard to respond to our own needs the way we can to others, isn't it? We can usually be more available to others than to ourselves.*

Take a moment to jot down all the skills you use to support a friend in need:

_____

_____

You have within you the perfect skills to meet your own unmet needs. There is no one else who can truly fill these holes.

Find one or more close friends and ask them what unique qualities and gifts you offer them when they are in need. Have them tell you about the times when you've demonstrated these qualities. As they are telling you about yourself, look into their eyes, without interrupting, and feel the truth of what they are saying. At the end of this exercise, limit your response to a simple "thank you." Try not to diffuse your feelings.

You might even be able to detect the parts of your body which hold on to your parents. Also, please notice how effective you are at taking in compliments.

During this exercise in which a friend is telling you about yourself, you might recall times when your parents were there for you in a similar manner. Sometimes our pain obscures our joy, with the hurts outweighing the love that we received. Healing happens when we remember and acknowledge everything. To see through new eyes is to see more of the whole story.

Pain and suffering are not exceptions to the human condition; they are inevitable players in the drama of our lives.
— Wayne Muller

YOUR CHILDREN

If you are a parent, you may want to guide your children through the Family Triangles. It is uncanny to see how frequently the unmet needs of the children are identical to those of the parents. A simple example might be that of a father who felt his own dad was not there for him. He might compensate by taking his kids surfing and skiing, when what his children really want is a father who is more emotionally present when they are speaking to him. His children need the same kind of father that he needed.

The most difficult part of going through the Family Triangles process with your children is refraining from interrupting them with explanations, and reasons why you haven't met their needs. Listen to your children and hear their truth, their reality, and so offer them the gift of your understanding, empathy, and acceptance. This might also offer you further insights into your own life. Through understanding why you are the way you are, you might understand why your parents were the way they were, which is another step on the way to forgiveness.

Summary

As human beings, we experience separation and individuation later than other species. Our childhood hurts may serve as the cutting of the emotional umbilical cord. No matter how painful or inappropriate these hurts may be, they often create essential boundaries and precipitate the process of differentiation and individuation.

*It is by turning away from our mothers that
we finally become, by our different paths,
grown men and women.*
— Joan Riviere

Though the father's role is sometimes overlooked as an important influence in shaping the child's psyche, it may be just as significant as the mother's. (This is especially true after the age of three.) However, due to the intrauterine experience, your attachment to your mother in the first few years of life was a powerful influence.* The prenatal experience holds a lifetime within itself.

Your hurts or unmet needs from both parents can be the prime movers of individuation, providing you with the people skills, vocational skills, and hidden gifts that now help you to serve others as well as yourself. Yet any needs that remain unfulfilled can become the sources of self-abuse, victimization, relational disharmony, and anger.

If we can silence our internal critics and treat ourselves as lovingly as we treat our friends, we can begin to heal ourselves and be kinder to those we love.

Often our hurts and unmet needs are identical to those of our parents. This fact alone does not diminish or negate our pain, nor should it. Understanding it may, however, diminish the blame. Our parents could not easily give us what was not given to them. Giving up the need to blame is the first step toward forgiveness.

If grief and pain are sometimes necessary for growth of the person, then we must learn not to protect people from them automatically as if they were always bad.

— Abraham Maslow

---

*Robert Karen, *Becoming Attached*.

Four

From Relationship
to Partnership

Lovers do not require from God any proof,
or any text, nor do they knock on a door
to make sure this is the right street.

— Rumi

A SUCCESSFUL CLOSE RELATIONSHIP either
starts as, or evolves into, a partnership. Unfortunately, many relationships end up focused on
differences and so are based on a certain amount
of friction, competition, and tension. Our intimate live-in relationships offer us a constant
reminder of the work we still have to do. If we are
successful, we can transform an ordinary relationship into the precious gift of partnership.

How does a relationship move from the early
courtship phase, through the difficult relationship phase, into a creative partnership?

Courtship brings out our playfulness. During
this phase there is often an intimate sharing,
where even parts of our shadow are sometimes
exposed as we test each other's degree of acceptance. Mixed in with these hidden parts are our
childhood gifts. Attracted to similar qualities in
each other, we feel a sense of belonging—a recognition of a familiar face of love. In courtship, we

tend to radiate a youthful joy that friends and family notice. We glow.

When courtship moves into marriage, or other forms of live-in relationship, things change. Living together recalls the family of origin. The honeymoon is soon over, as the unfinished business of the past turns fun into work. Each partner may now begin to wonder, Where did it go? Where the hell did the love go?

The relationship can then deteriorate into a chronic relationship, held together by tension and only momentary reminders of courtship feelings. Blame may arise, overt or insinuated. As the unmet needs from childhood again create dissatisfaction, the relationship may sink to the level of a "he said—she said" battle. Usually, the partners don't see how they are projecting their childhood unmet needs and their disowned (shadow) parts onto their mates. Then, as if by magic, the mates may even start acting out their partner's projection. In chronic relationships, we end up living with what we least like about ourselves, because that is what we see in the other person.

The work at this point is to surrender expectations and attachments, and to stop blaming. We can begin to move toward partnership and truly meet each other for the first time, as two unique individuals. As in any relationship or partnership, disagreements will continue to occur. There are times when major disagreements are best worked out separately, alone or with the help of a wise friend or knowledgeable therapist.

The heat of an argument can obscure the personal insights necessary for resolving a conflict. Time apart often helps us not only to recognize but to admit how we participate in causing friction. With awareness, empathy, and honesty, we can then reunite with our mates more creatively.

As we progress with our individual inner work, we move with greater and greater ease from feeling disconnected to reunion. We start to get more out of time alone *and* time together. The relationship becomes a place to *play*, to relish whatever is happening in the moment, and to create works of love that serve others. It becomes a partnership. In a partnership there is a commitment to embracing pain as well as joy. The real gift of partnership is the discovery of play.

Loneliness is an inevitable outcome of real love,
but it is also a process through which new love
becomes possible.
— Clark Moustakas

Let's look at the story of one couple. Roger and Diane are both therapists with a strong interest in using Family Triangles in their practice; therapists and other professional caregivers are not immune to interpersonal conflict!

Paul: *Tell me about the courtship phase of your relationship, when you first met.*
Roger: *We worked together for about a year before we got together as a couple. I was immediately drawn to Diane. I loved*

her aliveness, her intelligence, her beauty, and especially her vulnerability. I was a white knight, listening to her talk about her previous relationships and her abusive childhood.

Diane: *Roger was both my teacher and partner in the training. He gave me the space to make mistakes. I loved how gentle he was with criticism. I loved his sensuality, his willingness to listen to my horrific past, the dark stuff. Most importantly I felt heard. I loved the way he sounded, tasted, loved me—it was joy! I had never experienced anything like it. It was also kind of scary.*

Paul: *And what's happening now, since you've been married? It's about two years, isn't it?*

Diane: *Almost. Well, there is less sex, less willingness to talk about what's going on . . . less sharing. He seems less interested in what I'm feeling. Now I'm closing down—there is no joy.*

Paul: *Why are you feeling a need to close down?*

Diane: *I feel as if who I am is not good enough.*

Paul: *Roger, what's been happening for you since you got married?*

Roger: *I have less desire for sex. I feel less acceptable . . . like what I give is not enough. I feel criticized by Diane's questions about why we don't make love or communicate enough. When I hear those questions I feel afraid of being held to my answers. But I don't know the answers. We get into these cycles of joy and despair. We go from really good to really bad.*

Paul: *Diane, how do you take his nonresponsiveness to your questions?*

Diane: *It increases that "not being good enough" piece.*

Paul: *Let's look at your Triangles . . .*

Paul: *Diane, you always wanted to be acknowledged; and that happens to be one of Roger's gifts. I also imagine that your generosity makes Roger feel accepted.*

Diane: *I think that is what brought us together.*

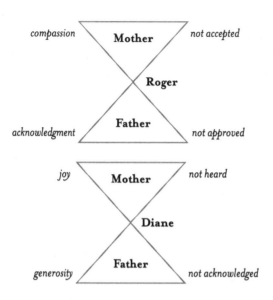

Paul: *What attracts us at first often seems to fade. Look, Diane, now that the courtship is over, you blame Roger for not bringing joy into the relationship, and for not being generous with sex. And, Roger, you blame Diane for not acknowledging you. You blame each other for your not getting the love you both feel entitled to. Sometimes we sabotage the familiar love of our childhood because we're afraid of experiencing the hurt that was attached to it.*

Diane: *I can see how I do that. Now when Roger is generous in his acknowledgment of me I tend to block it or tell him it is not enough.*

Paul: *Let's look at the relationship between the gifts and the hurts. Roger, both of your parents seem to be giving you mixed messages. Your gift of compassion from your mother is paradoxical with the hurt of nonacceptance. Usually, someone who is compassionate is accepting. Disparity also exists between your father's gift and hurt. The gift from your father is acknowledgment; and that is inconsistent with his lack of approval. An* inconsistency like this can create distrust in love. Roger, do you question Diane's love or feel she gives you mixed messages?

Roger: *Definitely. There are times I just don't believe what she says, how she feels, or even that she loves me.*

Paul: *I can see how that would make it difficult to answer her questions. You might feel as if they have some kind of hook in them. Let's look more closely at the combination of gifts and hurts. We tend to come out of our childhood expecting that our gifts automatically come with the same hurts. For example, Diane, you might unconsciously believe that joy occurs along with the experience of not being heard. Or Roger . . . that acknowledgment is accompanied by lack of approval. In fact, we often sabotage getting our gift because we don't want the pain that we expect with it.*

There may even be times, Roger, when you are being compassionate but you don't feel accepted. When you acknowledge Diane, you may feel that she doesn't give you approval. What's even more bizarre is that if Diane does give you acceptance and approval (the opposites of your hurts), you'll set it up so that compassion and acknowledgment are missing!

Diane: *That's for sure. Why does he do that?*

Paul: *Since compassion came from his mother without acceptance, he unconsciously believes that acceptance must come without compassion. The same is true about acknowledgment without approval. We imagine the two can't both be present if they weren't in childhood. That's what seems to happen, no matter how crazy it sounds. If someone heals your hurts, you unconsciously may think you'll lose your gifts. If someone offers the gifts, you'll think they will also re-create your hurts.*

Roger: *It's insane! How do I do it?*

Paul: *Good question! How do you do it with Diane?*

Roger (*thoughtful pause*): *By criticizing how she is not compassionate enough . . . or doesn't acknowledge me in the right* *way. I project my hurts of nonacceptance and lack of approval onto her.*

Diane: *That's true. But now I'm looking at what I do, too. I complain that he's not generous enough and that he doesn't know how to play or be joyful.*

Paul: *Look at your Triangles and see if you can really understand what you do.*

Diane: *It is clear that I project the opposite of my gifts onto him; which I just did a minute ago. And I set him up by either not hearing his joy or not acknowledging his generosity.*

Paul: *So, of your gifts, which one did each of you cherish most?*

Diane: *Generosity.*

Roger: *Acknowledgment.*

Paul: *Now let's explore the shadows of the gifts. What are their opposites?*

Diane: *The opposite of generosity is receiving.*

Roger: *The opposite of acknowledgment is neglect, which leads me to a sense of being unworthy.*

Paul: *Diane, your chief complaint to me about Roger was that you were feeling neglected by him—right? Roger, you said that she doesn't receive what you offer—what you give is not enough? Each of you is acting out the other's shadow—the opposite of the gifts! You have each projected your shadow on the other; and, in reality, what you are seeing is a mirror of yourself.*

Diane: *He's the one who doesn't feel "good enough," not me. I took that on.*

Roger: *Yes, but you always focus on what I am doing wrong— not on what you are doing.*

Paul: *Good! Now we have a new battle! Let's get back to the shadows of the gifts. Diane, what did you say is the opposite of your cherished gift of generosity?*

Diane: *Receiving. There are always strings attached.*

Paul: *Is there a gift in those strings?*

Diane: *Intimacy!*

Paul: *How can you have both intimacy and generosity in your life?*

Diane: *Hmmm . . . by giving up control. As long as I'm the giver, I'm in control.*

Paul: *Great! So true intimacy is found in both generosity and its shadow, receiving.*

Diane: *That's scary for me because of the abuse in my history. It seemed easier for me to surrender in the early part of our relationship, the courtship phase.*

Paul: *That's understandable. The experience of childhood abuse makes it really hard to let yourself lose control as an adult.*

Diane: *Well, I'm forty years old now. I am not saying I am not scared, but I feel ready to move on.*

Paul: *You both unconsciously took on each other's hurts and shadows. Let's try to get untangled. We might find an answer in the opposites of your cherished gifts. Roger, is there a gift in feeling neglected, unworthy? I believe you said that feeling neglected is the opposite of your most cherished gift, acknowledgment.*

Roger: *When people neglect me it means they leave me alone. I'm free!*

Paul: *So there is a hidden gift in the shadow.*

Roger: *Are you saying that I have a vested interest in not being accepted or not getting approval?*

Paul: *I don't know . . . do you?*

Roger: *I do crave freedom. My worst fear in life is dependency. I hate the word. But that leaves me with one foot in the relationship and one foot out.*

Paul: *So what happens when the two of you are in your other gifts: that is, when Roger is compassionate and Diane, you are in joy?*

Diane: *That's where we were in courtship.*

Roger: *Exactly! When she's in her joy I can't get enough of her!*

Diane: *Rog—when you're being compassionate, I melt.*

Paul: *We tend to move from courtship to chronic relationship when we settle into living from our cherished gifts. Then the blaming begins. He wants to be acknowledged for all that he's done for you and you want to be loved for your generosity. Let's take another look at the hurts. There are hidden gifts in the hurts. Roger, what are the gifts that might come from nonacceptance or lack of approval?*

Roger (without hesitation): *Freedom. I am back into my need for freedom.*

Paul: *What is the hidden gift for you, Diane, in not being heard and not being acknowledged?*

Diane: *It's also freedom. That is just what I projected onto him.*

Paul: *Your mutual need for freedom is getting in the way of intimacy. How can you have both freedom and intimacy?*

Diane (long pause): *Maybe by balancing our need to be alone with our need for togetherness.*

Paul: *Absolutely! Both of you have an unconscious need for freedom, and a conscious desire for intimacy. They only seem to be in conflict. If you can admit your need for freedom; while also appreciating intimacy, you might bring them into balance.*

The important thing is that you now have more choice. You are mirrors of each other, and when you begin to see the unconscious games that you play, you will make more creative choices in responding to each other.

Roger: *How do we do this?*

Paul: *First, bring your cherished gift into balance by embracing the shadow—the opposite of the gift. Also bring your other gifts back into the relationship. Those are the gifts that attracted you to each other. For Diane, it's your joy, and Roger, it's your compassion.*

Second, meet your own needs. Do your own work to take care of your childhood hurts. Take responsibility and stop blaming each other. Be willing to state your needs, but realize that they don't have to be met by your partner for your happiness.

Third, play more. Let pain and joy in and out as rapidly as possible. Live fully in each moment. Play with the gifts you love in each other. Enjoy the freedom and security that can be found in both aloneness and togetherness.

And finally, when things are breaking down, go into aloneness long enough to see your part of what's happening. Take back your projections. Acknowledge the person opposite from you as your mirror, your mirror for love and your mirror for healing. When you can appreciate the truth of this, come together again and share your insights. Openness and honesty are synonymous with intimacy.

Your relationship points to the work that needs to be done, but at times it may need to be done apart from your mate, especially when it involves anger and blame. This might mean working it through with a trusted friend or therapist.

Partnership is a dance between two whole people who are not afraid to expose every inch of themselves to each other. It's a dance between two people who feel comfortable in both aloneness and togetherness. It's a dance of individuation and sharing. The goal of life is partnership—partnership not only with our mates but with all of life. This is the source of true compassion.

As we have seen, the childhood experience of love and pain is difficult to understand. In the attempt to create meaning out of this paradox, the child can make wrong assumptions that have long-term consequences. One assumption is that certain gifts always come at the cost of certain hurts or unmet needs; another is that love hurts or that love cannot be trusted. As a child, you might have thought you were unworthy or unlovable. These assumptions become the basis of your adult reality.

Let's look again at the whole picture of your childhood gifts and hurts. Look for paradoxes: between the gifts, for example (creating a kind of paralysis), or between the hurts (creating a sense of victimization, no matter what happens). Can you see the source of some of your own assumptions?

The field of psychiatry is the field of interpersonal relationships . . . a personality can never be isolated from the complex of interpersonal relationships in which the person lives and has his being.

— Harry Stack Sullivan

If you experienced a repetition of painful events in your childhood, powerful memory patterns were probably stored for retrieval at a later date. Any similar event that matches even a trace of a given memory can recall the entire emotional charge associated with that memory.* This phenomenon is one source of post-traumatic stress syndrome. Remembering emotional and physical pain has been a key to our survival as a species; unfortunately, this kind of instant recall can be a real obstacle to intimacy. We all make

---

*Paul Brenner, Robert Livingston, and John Weeks, "Chronic Pain and Its Management."

inaccurate assumptions at times, and these distort our reality.

Have you ever unconsciously sabotaged a relationship rather than risk losing the parental gift, or the gift hidden in the hurt?

Let's briefly look again at Roger's gift of compassion from his mother, with the hurt of not being accepted. If Diane accepted him, he assumed that she would not be compassionate. Along with her acceptance, he may have felt a loss of freedom and a sense of dependency. He usually either discounted her or disconnected from the relationship through blame, criticism, or some other defense mechanism.

As children, if we had two separate but simultaneous experiences, we tended to assume that they were linked. We then came to expect this combination to be repeated elsewhere in life. If one part of the equation is missing, we assume the other is missing, too. If one is present, we assume the other is present. Our gifts and hurts became fused, and are now the source of our relationship themes and patterns, especially in long-term relationships.

Commitment, intimacy, and live-in situations are reminders of our childhood experience in the family. Here is where we begin to sabotage our relationships. The most common internal voice that comes up to help re-create our family experience is the inner critic, often projecting our shadow onto our partner. This might be when we start telling ourselves that we'd be better off alone.

I am convinced that much of what we now call
psychology is the study of the tricks we use to
avoid the anxiety of absolute novelty by making
believe the future will be like the past.
— Abraham Maslow

Live-in relationships become chronic when we blame the relationship for not giving us what we want. We often use our intimate relationships to perpetuate and justify our distrust of love. We won't escape our past until we begin to look at and question our childhood assumptions.

We sometimes like ourselves more when we're alone than when we're in a long-term relationship. The paradox of this is like saying, "you should be with me when I am alone!" It may seem as though our partners never see us at our best. However, if you have someone in your life who can meet your needs and you can avoid sabotaging the relationship, then you have already started the work of self-repair. In meeting your own needs, you can now allow another person into your life without the fear of losing your gifts.

Suffering ceases to be suffering when one has a
clear precise picture of it.
— Baruch Spinoza

You may discover that your family patterns and childhood assumptions don't play themselves out in intimate relationships as much as in your work or with your kids. The chronic relationship can rear its head in many different arenas, and in many different ways. Remember that what you see in your mate, your children, and your coworkers may be yourself. When you can begin to laugh at what once would have angered you, you are on the road to breaking unconscious patterns. This is true freedom.

InSights

Look back at your Family Triangles Map on pages 25 and 50 and transpose them on to page 91.

Are or were you "married" to your mother, your father, a combination of both, or parts of each?

_____

_____

Can you find characters at work or in old relationships that match parts of your Triangles?

_____

_____

Does one of your children trigger or upset you more than another?

_____

_____

If it appears that your present relationships no longer re-create your childhood scenario, then you can give yourself credit for growth, understanding, and healing.

How do you see yourself at least beginning to change old patterns and jump off your own karmic wheel?

_____

_____

The deeper a soul-connection goes, however, the more it brings our karmic patterns and personal neuroses to the surface.
— John Welwood

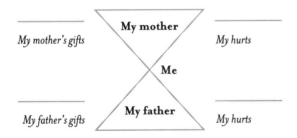

Notes

Perhaps we continually replay our childhood scenarios until we begin to see differently enough to change the script. Look at how this can happen.

What do your chronic relationships look like?

_____

_____

_____

What are you looking for in a loving relationship?

_____

_____

_____

What happens for you when life answers your prayers?

_____

_____

_____

How do you sabotage life's gift?

_____

_____

_____

Notes

Most of us have an unconscious "formula" for our relationships, as a result of assuming that our childhood gifts and hurts are inevitably linked.

For example: Jim is an artist. Jim's gift from his father was honesty. The unmet need from his father was to be appreciated. Now, when Jim asks his wife to look at his work, if she says it's good, he thinks she's not being honest, and he doesn't believe her. If she says anything critical, he believes she's being honest.

Jim's gift—hurt formula:

honesty = lack of appreciation; therefore,
appreciation = dishonesty

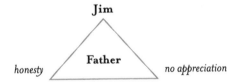

My gifts are

_____

Therefore I expect my hurts to be

_____

In an intimate relationship, when I am offered the opposite of my hurt—that is, when my need is being met—I imagine I'll lose my gift by

_____

_____

_____

```
      _____          My mother          _____
    My mother's gifts       \  /            My hurts
                             \  /
                              \/
                              /\ Me
                             /  \
      _____              /    \          _____
    My father's gifts    My father          My hurts
```

DISTRUST FROM THE GIFT AND THE HURT

Receiving both a gift and a hurt from a significant caregiver is experienced by the child as a mixed message. The paradox that both love and pain can come from the same parent inevitably leads to some degree of distrust: "How can my parent both love me and hurt me?" A child usually doesn't see that love and pain are separate events that can coexist at times but needn't always. The ultimate conclusion the child comes to is, "I can't trust love," or "I'm unlovable."

Such distrust is even greater when the gift and hurt seem truly incompatible. When asked, "What is your father's gift?" you might reply, "He was so accepting." What a paradox if, when asked, "What was your father's hurt?" you replied, "He was critical of me!" This kind of paradox is quite common, and can lead to the kind of constant distrust found in many codependent relation-ships. In a codependent relationship, one part-ner's needs are continually sacrificed in order to meet the other's. Unmet needs can perpetuate feelings of unworthiness and resentment.

Co-dependence is an agreement
between people to stay locked in
unconscious patterns.

— Gay and Kathlyn Hendricks

Our childhood experience of our family often penetrates our adult relationships. Our view of reality may be sharply defined by our childhood perceptions, which can lead to love, pain, distrust, fear, bonding, and self-fulfilling prophecies.

It has been said that, as children, we believe what we see; and as adults, we see what we believe. We see what we expect to see; we believe what we want to believe. The mixed messages that led to childhood distrust of a parent can be carried over as distrust of others of that gender as an adult. And if the child is of the same sex as the parent, this can lead to distrust in oneself.

As one client explained: "My father was very accepting at times, yet at other times critical. Maybe that explains why I have trouble trusting other men, and myself as well. I often think of Groucho Marx saying that he wouldn't join any club that would take him as a member."

Recall Sally, who came to us to deal with the effects of distrust in her work and personal life. The gift and hurt from her mother—always being there, and lack of protection—are contradictory. Sally had a hard time trusting women in general, and certainly herself. And she tended to project that distrust onto others, imagining that they were suspicious of her. She was constantly suspicious of others being suspicious! This caused her a lot of stress at work.

Sally's gift and hurt from her father were also contradictory. One time he gave her the gift of listening, whereas most of the time he was disrespectful and verbally abusive. Sally could see how this paradox might have led to her basic distrust of men. She began to see how distrust was a major theme in her life, one that she now wanted to change.

Even her habitual posture (head turned a little to one side) expressed distrust. We experimented with this, by having Sally slowly turn her head from the side to face someone directly, and to pay attention to what this brought up for her. It was powerful and surprising for her to feel how much her habitual head position sustained the feeling of distrust. Becoming aware of her body in this way was one step toward developing more trust. She began to see trust as a choice, not just a feeling.

Please look at your Family Triangles again and see if the gifts and the hurts from either parent are incompatible. If they are, answer the following questions. Refer to page 96.

Can you see how distrust has affected your view of reality?

_____

_____

Has it made it difficult to trust others, or yourself?

_____

_____

Do you have more trust issues with one gender than the other?

_____

_____

Do you trust yourself?

_____

_____

Notes

BONDING

If the hurt of one parent is healed by the gift of the other, it can lead to a bond with the healing parent and a tendency to bond with others of that gender.

Stan is an example: "The gift of my father was intimacy; the hurt was criticism. The gift of my mother was freedom; the hurt was that she was not available."

Stan's father's gift of intimacy healed his mother's unavailability. Therefore, he tends to bond more easily with men. In his words, "I hang out with the guys—I'll defend my buddies to my dying day."

Look now at your own Family Triangles to see if one parent's gift balances or heals the other's hurt. Distrust and bonding for one or the other gender affect our intimate relationships and are frequently acted out in the workplace.

DIVORCE AND AFFAIRS

Have you ever felt that your partner was too good to be true, or had thoughts like, "They're a better person than I am . . . I don't know why they married me"? Such questions may conceal a sense of unworthiness. The difference between your perception of your mate's goodness and your own low self-worth can lead, in extreme cases, to divorce, affairs, or compulsive acting-out behavior such as sexual or substance addiction. The divorce, affair, or addiction might be a way that you prove your unworthiness to yourself and others.

Listen to Charles's story:

Charles: *I'm addicted. Every time I'm away on a business trip, I'm either looking to get laid or find myself in porn shops. I hate myself for it!*

Paul: *Is your wife aware of this?*

Charles: *We've discussed it. She's the greatest. They don't come any better. I don't know why she hangs in with me. After I get home, I love her more than ever. But of course she's losing her patience. Either she's going to leave, or I'll have to! I can't stand myself as it is now.*

In Charles's attempt to preserve his wife's goodness, he diminishes his own, and in time sets himself up for separation or divorce. His fear becomes a self-fulfilling prophecy.

Life meets us where we are. The goodness we see in others, as with other qualities, also exists in us. Yet we can rarely see it. We do a disservice to ourselves, and to those we love, by not appreciating all of our parts, especially our goodness. Believing that goodness lies in others is as much of a projection as believing that blame does.

I increased the world's guilt and anguish, by
doing violence to myself, by not daring to walk
toward my own salvation. The way to salvation
leads neither to the left nor the right. It leads
into your heart, and there alone is God, and
there alone is peace.

— Hermann Hesse

Summary

When your family of origin infiltrates your adult relationships, the true meaning of love is limited. These limitations can affect your actions, your relationships, your vocation, and your entire worldview.

Seeing Your Life Through New Eyes will give you the option to be less reactive, to respond more consciously, to exercise your inherent right to be creatively free in the moment—to be a whole, self-actualized, functional human being. You can begin not only to see your own wholeness, but also to accept and appreciate the beauty in others.

We become aware of our own autonomy, our own identification. We find out who we really are. And having made the discovery we are ready for the love and service of others.
—Thomas Merton

One purpose of relationship is to do the work of healing ourselves and each other. The gift of partnership is to be of service to others, to play, and to enjoy life. In play there is no expectation, no distrust, no blame. True play invites us to simply experience the moment, accepting life as a game.

Partnership is governed by the law that it takes two to say "yes," or one to say "no." "Yes" is the key word for establishing mutual openness, vulnerability, and intimacy. A "no" rules a "yes." "No" is the key word to establishing boundaries when aloneness is desired. Love is not a matter of constant intimacy or closeness; love swings between togetherness and aloneness. Security in partnership is found in the balance.

We recommend that you take a break before moving on to the next chapter on pain, fear, and coping. Use this time for further insights into past and present relationships.

In a nutshell, differentiation is the process by which we become more uniquely ourselves by maintaining ourselves in relationship with those we love. . . . It's a process—a lifelong process of taking our own "shape."

— David Schnarch

Five

Pain, Fear, and Coping

There is a way of breathing that's a shame and a suffocation.
And there's another way of expiring,
a love-breath,
that lets you open infinitely.

— Rumi

IF AS CHILDREN WE FEEL HURT REPEATEDLY, it can lead to the pain of abandonment or abuse. The pain of abandonment is the feeling of being neglected, left alone, or deserted. The pain of abuse is the result of inappropriate or hurtful contact with someone more powerful; this can take the form of physical, emotional, or mental abuse.

The repeated pain of abandonment, over time, can take us to a fear of aloneness, while the repeated pain of abuse, over time, can lead to a fear of togetherness, of intimacy, of relationship.

Kay: *The hurt from my mother—her not being there—made me feel abandoned and neglected. The hurt I felt from my father was criticism. It felt abusive. I didn't know where to hide to be safe.*
Paul: *Can you see any connection between these painful feelings and your adult relationships?*
Kay: *I wonder if this is why I don't know whether to hold on to someone, or run away. When I'm intimate with someone, I am*

afraid that they'll leave me. At the same time, I am afraid of being abused.

Kay felt abandoned by one parent and abused by the other. Now, when she is in a relationship, she wants out; when she is out, she wants in. This historical paradox can keep her in the midst of pain and fear.

What would happen if you felt abandoned by both parents? You might either tend to cling to your relationships addictively, or to give up on relationships altogether because aloneness is so familiar. On the one hand, the addictive relationship—"I'll do anything to make this relationship work!"—can lead to loss of self, the ultimate abandonment. On the other hand, you may set up yourself or your partner to end the relationship: at least, in aloneness, you have learned to survive, if not thrive. Whether you hang on or leave, you will end up in the same place—alone.

And if you have felt abused by both parents? You may prefer to avoid relationships. Or you may choose an abusive relationship because it is so familiar; love is fused with pain. Either scenario leads to more pain.

By seeing your life through new eyes, you can begin to bring what was unconscious into consciousness. In so doing, the old patterns that have repeated themselves throughout your life can shift and give way to new and more nourishing experiences.

Look now at your childhood hurts to see if they play out in your adult relationships in terms of abandonment or abuse. Refer to page 96. (Where we have offered multiple choices, please circle one.)

The hurt of my mother led to the pain of
    abandonment   abuse   both

The hurt of my father led to the pain of
    abandonment   abuse   both

The pain I experienced from my mother led to the fear of
    aloneness   intimacy   both

The pain I experienced from my father led to the fear of
    aloneness   intimacy   both

My biggest fear in an intimate relationship is

_____

_____

And when this happens, my usual reaction is to

_____

_____

I would prefer to respond by

_____

_____

Notes

Fear, like pain, lives on as memory. Fear can make your nightmare expectations come to life. Fear persists in silence, or is heard within as a haunting voice, crying "Run! . . . Avoid! . . . Hold on! . . . Look out!" Fear creates a strategic persona: the seducer or the rejecter, the attacher or the avoider, the engager or the disengager.

What you fear is usually what was painful about your past. Through fear, you continue to project your past onto the present. Not only do you lose the present, but your future can become an ongoing replay of the past.

This kind of fear is like a "black hole," which swallows everything that comes near it yet is never filled. Although we may ask others to try to fill this hole—to meet our needs and stop our fears— we usually set them up to fail. To bring more brightness into our personal lives we need to stop, turn around, and face the darkness. In so doing, we have the opportunity to see our life in a new light. We can find out that we have the power to reprogram our perceptions, our responses, and therefore our experiences. But first, we must look at what keeps this show running—our habitual coping skills.

Coping Skills

By age seven, when the child can compare some
properties of self with those of others, he
generates either a motive of hostility toward, or
a motive for acceptance by, those peers who
possess desired characteristics he does not have.
— Jerome Kagan

Coping skills—such as being a loner, a rebel, a pleaser, a jokester, and so on—move us through life without revealing our hurts to others. We created these strategies in childhood in an attempt to protect ourselves from pain and fear. Our inherent genetic temperament probably has even more influence on our choice of a coping style than our appreciation of our gifts. We tend to move into coping whenever our safety needs are greater than our needs for growth.

Because our coping skills were initially designed to control what we as children saw as a hostile or uncaring environment, these strategies temporarily helped us to live in the security of our gifts, while trying to protect us from our hurts. Coping skills helped us survive as children. Yet these same strategies, when they become habitual, can become self-destructive in adulthood.

Over time, our strategic responses tend to become automatic, reflexive, unconscious habits of behavior, and as a result they limit us. Habitual reactions don't give us a choice, and choice is freedom. Without conscious choice we are trapped in an endless replay of the past, like Bill Murray's weatherman in the movie *Groundhog Day*, where every day was a repetition of the previous one. Eventually, his main wish in life was for difference and change; he finally found salvation in changing his old attitudes and ways of coping.

As children, our perception that we needed to control or manipulate our surroundings marked the loss of our innocence: paradise lost. The skills we then used to accomplish this control provided us with the illusion of safety from our fears. We learned either to engage—to draw people toward us—out of a fear of abandonment, or to disengage—withdraw from or reject others— in fear of abuse. At times we may even have used a combination of engagement and disengagement—attachment and detachment—seduction and then rejection.

Although our pleasing skills—being humorous, sensitive, caring, helpful, an achiever, and so on—appear to be socially acceptable and different from our rejecting skills—being rebellious, independent, withdrawn, confrontational—they are similar in that they are both used to create a safe environment.

Coping skills were, at first, the only way that we had to creatively respond to life's pain—the strategies we developed to get others to meet our needs, or to not feel the pain of our needs going unmet. Many of our coping skills, along with our people skills, have become our gifts to life, and may even serve us in our vocation.

Although coping skills are essential for ego development, they can congeal into an identity, one which armors us against feeling. These skills are created from sheer endurance, perseverance, and doing our damnedest to survive. Through repetition, the skills can become our modus operandi and be confused with our sense of self. They identify us to ourselves and to others; we forget that this is how we learned to survive, and avoid pain. In time, we imagine that this is who we really are, who we were intended to be. Sometimes coping skills numb our feelings, and dampen our aliveness. As childhood ends, so does our trust in our intuition and instincts.

When our childhood strategies become ingrained and connected to our survival, we may become unwilling or afraid to change. Unfortunately, most of our coping skills tend to re-create our childhood pain and hold us in the abyss of our unmet needs. For example, independence and self-reliance—admirable traits—that were developed in childhood in response to a father or mother who "just wasn't there," can eventually re-create the childhood hurt of loneliness. You may disengage by rejecting help, or by becoming self-sufficient in order not to feel your pain. You may give others the impression that you don't need anyone else, while inside you lives a very lonely person who craves intimacy, but who can't seem to let others in. When this happens, your child of the past is controlling your adult of the present. Coping skills are often based on a fear of losing relationship; in the end, however, relationships are too often lost as a result of our unconscious addiction to coping.

Meanwhile, the "I don't need you!" begun
as a rageful, wounded pout, now becomes
an unconscious stance toward people in
general, even loved people. This too is a
form of self starvation.
— Robert Karen

Here is a similar example, but with an opposite response to the hurt of a parent who was "not there": Ann was a motherless child, so she befriended her friends' mothers. They loved her. Ann became the "world's greatest pleaser." Past forty years old, Ann continued to be a pleaser. She finally sought help after a breakdown, finding herself repeatedly crying, "What about me? There's never anyone there for *me!*" She was so busy meeting everyone else's needs that she never allowed others to meet hers. The child who felt deprived became a self-deprived adult.

The child, faced with a difficult
choice between his own delight experiences
and the experience of approval from
others, must generally choose approval
from others, and then handle his
delight by repression or letting it die,
or not noticing it or controlling
it by willpower. . . .

If the only way to maintain the self is to lose others, then the ordinary child will give up the self.

— Abraham Maslow

In another example, Lenny withdrew in order to avoid feeling the pain of the lack of intimacy in his family: no touching, no hugging, nothing at all. In time, by retreating and not sharing any inner feelings, desires, or needs for physicality, he seemed to have quelled the pain of lack of intimacy. However, by adulthood, his habits of withdrawal and avoidance kept him from the intimacy he craved. The adult Lenny was again living with the boy's childhood pain.

Skills of both attachment (fear of aloneness) and rejection (fear of intimacy), when taken to an extreme, often lead to a complete loss of self, or to isolation. Opposites, taken to extremes, can end up in similar places. In either case, the end result can be chronic depletion and illness.

If, instead of hiding behind our coping skills, we are willing to redirect the ones that no longer work for us by healing the pain that created them (which came from the unmet needs), these very same skills can help us to rediscover our true selves. This will mark a significant change—giving up the obsessive need to manipulate. We can then begin to live more authentically, inspired from within rather than impelled to try to control our external world. We can still use the skills we originally developed for coping; they are part of our reservoir of strengths and responses. But we are no longer identified by them, and limited to them in every situation.

Ann, for example, developed many important skills related to pleasing others when she befriended her friends' mothers: helpfulness, responsibility, cooperation, and communication. These could serve her well, both at work as a receptionist in a dental care office, and at home, as long as they were balanced by healthy boundaries and taking care of her own needs as well. Then, her helpfulness and pleasing would arise not from the need to be loved, as they did when she was a child, but rather from the pleasure it would give her to be of service to others. It is simply doing the right thing for the right reason. Seduction and rejection are childhood games.

InSights

Let's look at your coping skills.

As a child, when I felt the hurt of my mother, I would

_____

to avoid feeling the pain. This is the way I coped.

As a child, when I felt the hurt of my father, I would

_____

to avoid feeling the pain. This is the way I coped.

How do my coping skills re-create the original pain of my child-hood?

From the hurt from my mother:

_____

_____

From the hurt from my father:

_____

_____

Are my coping skills paradoxical?

_____

_____

You will find that others may have difficulty trusting you if you have paradoxical or opposite coping strategies. Sue, for example, coped with one parental hurt by pleasing, and with the other by withdrawing. People often felt that they had to tiptoe around her mood swings. She behaved in relationships like a "rocking chair," sometimes leaning forward, into the relationship; at other times tipping backward, out of the relationship. Her coping strategies, pleasing and withdrawing, involved moving towards others at times, and pulling away at other times.

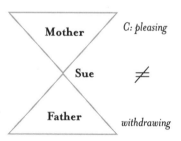

People might also distrust you if your gifts or people skills (opposites of hurts) are incompatible with your coping skills. Helen's gift from her father was service; he was always there. And her mother's hurt of criticism created the opposite, her people skill of accepting others. Yet her coping strategy for a mother who was critical was self-reliance and withholding. She often gave mixed messages that confused others. At times she seemed solitary and aloof, while at other times, she was very available.

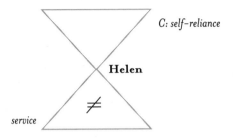

C: self-reliance

Helen

≠

service

Jody received the gift of emotional closeness from her mother. On the other hand, she developed a coping strategy of intellectualizing to deal with her mother's unreasonableness. Her husband and children never knew whether Jody would empathize or philosophize when they expressed their feelings. Were her responses going to be warm and compassionate, or cold and calculating?

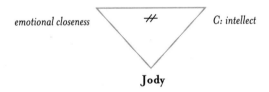

emotional closeness   ≠   C: intellect

Jody

Ask yourself whether one of your gifts or people skills is paradoxical with one of your preferred coping skills; or whether any of your two gifts, coping skills, or people skills are paradoxical with each other. Are you unconsciously giving mixed messages because of all the combinations and permutations of your unique gifts, people skills, and coping skills? If so, this can lead others to distrust you. They might never know who's going to show up when they're with you.

Your Self-Portrait

*But then what is your myth—the myth in
which you do live?*
— Carl Jung

Your self-portrait is a composite of the gifts you
received from your parents, your people skills,
and the coping skills you developed in response to
your hurts. The self-portrait is the mask we present to others. It is how we see ourselves and how
others see us. It can also be a facade to hide our
pain, our fear, and our shame. When we imagine
that parts of ourselves are not lovable or acceptable and so must remain hidden, we feel ashamed.

Our mask, our self-portrait, is more evident
in some situations than others, and often most
apparent in new relationships and at work. We
designed this mask to serve others as well as ourselves, yet this identity construct can cost us our
personal freedom and create a false sense of personal security.

Our self-portrait defines us. It becomes our
identity. We think it is who we are, instead of rec-
ognizing it as just a part of the whole. If I am
identified with being helpful to others to such a
degree that I can't say no, I limit myself to a way
of being that will eventually exhaust me. In
another example, Rose was having stress-related
digestive problems due to her work. She identified herself by saying, "I'm a lover, not a fighter!"
As a child, she had learned to cope with an angry,
unpredictable, and abusive parent by being a

mediator, and by keeping the peace. It meant she learned to avoid conflict at all costs. This made it impossible for her to set good boundaries at work by saying "no" when the demands were unfair. Instead, she suppressed her frustration and became sick. To behave any differently would have demanded that she redefine herself as a person.

The idea of change can be frightening. We might alter our masks during various stages of life, depending on what we are willing to reveal to particular individuals at different times. Most of us limit ourselves to only a few ways of being. Why do we choose to be less when we know, deep down, that we are more?

Now, think about how you define yourself based on your gifts, coping skills, and people skills. Your self-portrait may hide the hurts from your mother and father and how they shape your life. It can also hide the shadow of your most cherished gift, as well as the gifts hidden in the hurts.

All habits, defenses and coping mechanisms are doubtful and ambiguous since they are based on past experiences. Only the flexibly creative person can really manage [the] future, only the one who can face novelty with confidence and without fear. . . .

By protecting himself against the hell within himself, he also cuts himself off from the heaven within.

— Abraham Maslow

THE SHADOW OF YOUR SELF-PORTRAIT

No matter how fast you run,
your shadow more than keeps up.
Sometimes, it's in front!
— Rumi

Throughout much of this book, you have looked at different parts of your shadow. Now we'll find out where your shadow lives. Lurking behind your self-portrait are: the opposites of your gifts, the hurts, the pain, the fear, the distrust, the internalized parents, the controller, the critic, the victim, the perpetrator, the saboteur. . . all the shame.

Your shadow is that part of you that you think is unacceptable and that you don't want others to see.* You might even refuse to acknowledge it yourself. It keeps your story line going and directs your life from the inside out; it can be the motivation to seek change. The shadow is what drives you to heal, to evolve, and to live more authentically. The shadow cries out: "I am no longer willing to live in this limited box of my self-portrait, my false self!" To be whole, to be fully human and free, we must own our shame in order to transform it. We must make what has been unconscious conscious.

The negativity you feel toward your hidden parts is too often projected as blame—onto those you love as well as those you hate. You will tend to either blame or adore those who mirror whatever you are unwilling to recognize within yourself.

---

*Jung, *The Undiscovered Self.*

We have first to penetrate courageously
into the pit of our lower unconscious in
order to discover the dark forces that
ensnare and menace us.
— Robert Assagioli

ADDICTION

The limiting self-definition you carry out of child-hood can also lead to various forms of addictive behavior. Addictions are habitual behaviors with life-limiting or life-damaging consequences. A habit of withdrawing, for example, becomes an addiction when it happens automatically, even at times when you would rather be in a relationship than alone. Drugs and other substances, such as alcohol and food, can help a person withdraw in a more drastic way.

In many cases the intense and sometimes
overpowering craving for drugs, alcohol, food,
sex, or other objects of addiction is really a
misplaced yearning for wholeness, a larger
sense of self, or God.
— Christina and Stanislav Grof

Since childhood, all of us have developed strategies to ensure that our needs will be met. Our strategies have evolved from a set of creative responses to life, responses that grew out of our family situation, our earliest relationships, our developing sense of self, our temperament, and the ways in which we sought to obtain love. These strategies often become habits, and so they have the potential to be destructive to ourselves and to others, because we tend to use them in every situation, whether or not they are appropriate.

Our addictions affect our family, our social activities, our health, and our work. Denial is the hallmark of addiction, and addictions are the major obstacles to creativity. When we have the courage to live creatively, we find this to be the true antidote to addiction.

Some of us have tried to hold on to our old ideas and the result was nil until we let go absolutely. . . . Half measures availed us nothing.
— Alcoholics Anonymous

The gifts, hurts, and coping skills that create our self-portrait make up our most unconscious addictions. Because the gifts are what we cherished most about our parents, they become what we are convinced we need in our lives. We developed our coping skills in response to the pain of our childhood. They are designed to protect us from more pain and suffering. Quite simply, we are addicted to love and to avoiding pain.

Addiction to Your Self-Portrait

Here's an example of an addiction to childhood gifts:

Robert had been married three times and was a father of two. He was unconsciously addicted to his mother's gift of freedom and his father's gift of excitement: "I just have difficulty staying married. I always seem to feel suffocated." Robert often found relief from intimate relationships by having affairs that seemed to provide him with the gifts of his childhood. Eventually, he came for therapy feeling quite depressed and lonely. Multiple sexual partners had given Robert what he craved most: his gifts of excitement and freedom. However, his sexual addiction was also destroying his life and preventing him from healing his unmet need—intimacy. Robert's sexual addiction came out of his attempt to hold on to his childhood gifts and hurts.

Here's an example of an addiction to childhood hurts:

Jane was raised by a nanny. The gift from her mother was caring. Yet, her hurt was from her mother's absence. Her father's gift was kindness, but he, too, was often unavailable. Clearly, the gifts of both parents were paradoxical with the hurts. As you will remember, this can lead to childhood distrust. Jane recognized that the gift in the hurt of unavailable parents was her carefreeness; it was a carefreeness her parents could not control, and which led to many unpleasant experiences for them.

As coping skills, Jane learned how to please others and to be socially adept. During her

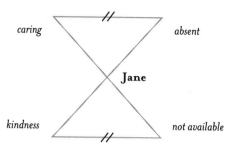

caring

absent

Jane

kindness

not available

teenage years, she developed an eating disorder, alternating between bulimia and anorexia. Jane was taken to various physicians and clinics to try to change these behaviors. However, anorexia and bulimia provided her with the attention from her parents that she so dearly craved. In adulthood, as a professional model, Jane continued to have bouts of anorexia and bulimia that went largely unnoticed: "It's just part of my profession." Jane's profession and social skills provided her with some of the same attention she sought as a teen. At the same time, important needs continued to go unmet.

In time, her eating disorder became a threat to her life: "I swear to God, I want to start eating again. I just don't know how to do it. I go into a trance. Each meal, I start out believing I can eat the food on my plate—I really *want* to do it! But the minute I see it before me, I think of ways to pretend I'm eating it, or to distract others from watching me hide it, or else I eat and regurgitate it within an hour. Yet I enjoy cooking and watching others eat."

Jane acknowledged the resentment she felt toward her nanny and blamed her parents for being unavailable to her in childhood. After intense inner work, she found a key to what she called the "black box" in the center of her mind. Inside the black box was a horrific raging force. Finally, after much soul-searching, she labeled the contents of the black box as "revenge." Anorexia started as unconscious revenge for her parents' absence and was rewarded with attention.

The challenge for Jane was that, over time, the revenge had assumed its own identity—separate from her own inner authority. Not only did this part not listen to her plea to eat, it also limited her carefreeness, something that the authority of her parents was never able to do! Jane found that recovery was a slow, day-by-day process of working through and making peace with her self-created parts.

Even if someone has a sincere desire to change a destructive behavior, there is often a self-created identity that resists the authority of its creator—the person who now wants to overcome the addiction. Addiction is like a snake biting its tail. It is true that addiction may have a genetic component, but responsibility for its manifestation must be assumed by the individual. The addict is both a victim and a perpetrator.

Here's an example of an addiction to pain:

Ellen was brought up in an abusive family. The strategy she used to avoid being treated unkindly by her father was to withdraw. This coping skill of withdrawal led Ellen into states of pain and loneliness: "I often felt isolated—trapped in my pain." In order to escape these feelings, she started to use cocaine: "Marijuana was too much of a downer, as was alcohol. Coke did it for me, even though, when I came down, my body was whacked." Cocaine ultimately recreated the abuse she experienced in childhood. The habit of being in pain was the real addiction. Cocaine became part of Ellen's unconscious way of substituting substance abuse for her abusive father.

WHEN YOUR SELF-PORTRAIT BREAKS DOWN

What is it that pushes someone over the line between habituation and addiction? Sometimes the line is crossed when the personal profile—the self-portrait—collapses.

Jason, a successful CEO, was raised in an affluent family. Describing what he appreciated most about his mother, he said: "She was exciting to be with." And for his father: "He was loyal." The hurt he felt from his mother was a lack of closeness, while his father was overly critical.

The coping skills Jason developed in response to his mother's lack of closeness were social graces. To avoid the pain of his father's criticism, he kept busy and became an achiever.

After retirement, Jason's coping skills of busyness, achievement, and social graces were no longer needed. The retirement gift of a crystal Tiffany bowl could not replace what he had suddenly lost. His identity collapsed. Retirement took away his gifts of loyalty to the firm he helped to build and the excitement that working provided. The only thing that remained of the old Jason was the pain of his own self-criticism and his profound sense of loneliness—his shame. His identity disintegrated within a month. Before Jason retired, he had been referred to as a social drinker. However, a few weeks after retiring, Jason became an uncontrollable alcoholic whose drinking bouts involved total blackouts. With the loss of his identity as a CEO, Jason had nothing left other than to live in his hurts. Alcoholism served to temporarily obscure those hurts, but between bouts the shame was intensified.

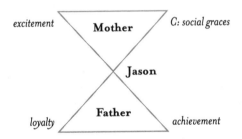

excitement   **Mother**   *C: social graces*

Jason

loyalty   **Father**   *achievement*

My Gifts   **My Copes**   **My People Skills**

Mother

Father

My Self Portrait

InSights

Your self-portrait might be leading to addictive behaviors.

When I look at my self-portrait, the aspects I cannot live without—my gifts, coping skills, and people skills—are

_____

_____

When I am afraid of losing those aspects, I act out by

_____

_____

My most likely choice of addiction (alcohol, work, sex, drugs, spending, and so on) would be

_____

A more creative and healthy choice would be

_____

The gifts I find in the upside of my hurts, which could enhance my life, are

_____

_____

The creative changes I can make in my life in order to diminish the likelihood of addictive behaviors are

_____

_____

*The hope is that by naming our own Chief
Feature we can learn to observe the many
ways in which this habit has gained control of
our lives. Then our neurotic skew of attention
can be enlisted as an ally whose presence
makes us suffer and causes us to remember
what we have lost.*

— Helen Palmer

Illness

If you look at your self-portrait, and take your
gifts, coping skills, and people skills to their
addictive extremes, you can imagine how they
might lead to emotional difficulties, such as pain,
depletion, entrapment, paralysis, boredom, loneliness, suffocation, or loss of self. In essence, all
of the states listed can lead to loneliness and loss
of self, and both loneliness and loss of self are
common precursors to illness. Group therapy has
been found to increase longevity in recovering
cancer and cardiac patients, through an enhanced
sense of connection and self-worth.*

When aspects of the personal profile created
by the gifts, coping skills, and people skills of
childhood are taken to an extreme, they can create health problems and addictions. Let's look at
an example:

---

*Lawrence LeShan, *Cancer as a Turning Point*; David Spiegel, *Living
Beyond Limits*; Dean Ornish, *Dr. Dean Ornish's Program for Reversing
Heart Disease*.

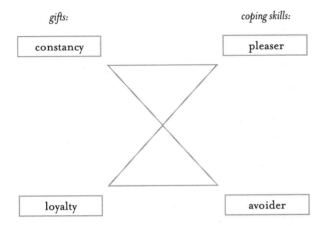

gifts:

constancy

coping skills:

pleaser

loyalty

avoider

Constancy, when taken to an extreme, can lead to boredom and emotional paralysis; being a pleaser can lead to loss of self and emotional depletion; being an avoider can lead to loneliness and paralysis; loyalty can lead to a sense of suffocation and entrapment.

Illness has been described as metaphor, and doing your Family Triangles can offer an insight into the sources of such illness.* It is not uncommon to see the identical complaints of paralysis, depletion, and loneliness in cases of chronic fatigue syndrome, fibromyalgia, and other musculoskeletal health problems. On the other hand, unresolved hurts of nonacceptance may lead to an autoimmune disease or even cancer. Is this a certainty? Absolutely not! But it is food for thought, if we are willing to view illness as metaphor, as the body's "computer readout" of the mind's dis-ease.

---

*Susan Sontag, *Illness as Metaphor*.

Our self-portrait hides our shame. We feel unworthy of love, which leads to feelings of self-abandonment and self-loathing. Our shame will not allow us to be fully loved. To love oneself is to radiate love to others. This happens effortlessly when we meet our own needs, break through the bonds of our Family Triangles, and move toward self-actualization.

◀ ▶ *InSights*

Now, look at your self-portrait to see what illnesses your gifts and coping skills—if taken to an extreme—might invite. Refer to page 131.

My mother's gift—to an extreme—can lead to

_____

And the corresponding coping skill can lead to

_____

My father's gift—to an extreme—can lead to

_____

And the corresponding coping skill can lead to

_____

Notes

We are not always responsible for creating our physical illnesses—we already have enough guilt and shame without needing to take on that burden, too. However, we are responsible—and therefore able to respond—to life's challenges. One way we can do this is by bringing our self-portrait into balance.

Just as we have associated love with pain, so, too, we have confused health and illness. Health is not the absence of disease. Health is the acceptance and the appreciation of oneself, of others, and of life. Emotional health cannot be separated from organic health.

We grow forward when the delights of growth and anxieties of safety are greater than the anxieties of growth and the delights of safety.
— Abraham Maslow

Summary

Your childhood pain and fear led to the unconscious development of coping skills that were designed to avoid pain and to help get your needs met. Coping skills mark the loss of innocence. These skills might obscure or distort the expression of your feelings. Over time, these same skills can become habitual, and even addictive, thus recreating your original unmet needs.

In a sense, your childhood stories serve that very purpose: they are how you hold on to your

parents and the status quo, and thus unknow-
ingly perpetuate your childhood insecurity. We
all feel most safe with what is familiar. "If the
hurt is not there, the parent is not there," says
the unconscious.

*Inner peace and contentment depend in large
measure upon whether or not the historical
family which is inherent in the individual can
be harmonized with the ephemeral conditions
of the present.*
— Carl Jung

Your coping skills, along with how you've
embodied the gifts from your parents, combine
to create an adult self-portrait that can hide a
plethora of disowned parts. The need to avoid
pain and to manipulate the environment
becomes addictive. What is sacrificed in the
process is *feeling*. To feel is to heal.

Healing begins by reclaiming your wholeness.
It was never lost; there is nothing missing; there
is no one to blame. Healing, then, is a process of
remembering and acknowledging wholeness. The
parts that need healing are those that are out of
balance, those that hide in the shadow.

The parts we need to reclaim for our wholeness are the ones that we have forgotten or disowned. There are many methods for reclaiming
disowned parts, including Voice Dialogue,
Internal Family Systems, the Hakomi Method,
and Gestalt therapy (see the resources in the

References for more information on these particular methods). Through such methods, disowned parts can be integrated into a unified whole. They may be disowned, but they have not been destroyed. Our disowned parts are trapped within the shadow of our self-portrait. What is hidden there has the potential to save us. These hidden parts are untapped treasures. In finding them, we often find forgiveness for our parents who, more than likely, experienced the same hurts and unmet needs.

In the words of Paul's father, Isadore Brenner, *you can't give someone a nickel if you don't have one.* Our parents could not meet our needs if their own had not been met. Our places of pain and emptiness are hand-me-downs. Are you old enough to have looked in the mirror only to see your parents staring back? In fact, everyone we meet offers a mirror, a mirror for our personal healing and awareness. We have reached a point in human development that gives us the wisdom and time for self-healing. Perhaps, in healing ourselves, we heal what the Hopi of the southwestern United States refer to as the "long body": the ancestors who have preceded our birth, our children, and those yet unborn.

How can a wise man, knowing the unity of life, seeing all creatures in himself, be deluded or sorrowful?

— Upanishads

Six

Our Calling

*Stretch your arms and take hold the cloth of your clothes
with both hands. The cure for pain is in the pain.
Good and bad are mixed. If you don't have both,
you don't belong with us.*

—Rumi

FROM OUR EARLIEST BEGINNINGS, life is a dance between detachment and reunification, separation and wholeness. From the moment the ascending sperm detach from their parent cells and begin their arduous and chaotic journey toward the descending, isolated, patiently waiting egg, there is a call to wholeness, a call to purpose, a gift to life.

Students of biology know that parthenogenesis, as seen in the whipped tailed lizard, is the development of an egg into a life form without fertilization. This amazing process gives birth to a clone of the mother. This phenomenon tells us that inherently the egg carries the blueprint for wholeness, for sameness, and for repeating the past. On the other hand, sperm are unable to reproduce themselves, yet in the process of fertilization they bring difference, newness, and change. Difference evolves into a new wholeness.*

---

*Paul Brenner, "The Biologic Origin of the Human Psyche."

Life is an ongoing journey that calls us to the repeated dance of detachment and reunification throughout our life cycle: birth and the cutting of the cord, integration into the family of origin and individuation, school associations and adolescent isolation, courtship, marriage, child-rearing, and death. Unfortunately, when we're unconscious of what moves us, our journey through life's events can keep us blind to our connection with all life and with our reason for being.

Our unique genetic makeup and family of origin were perfectly designed to serve life. What if our unique being as well as our unique journey become our unique gift to life? What if our greatest gift to life were found within our childhood hurts? What if the cosmic joke was for all of us to have been denied what we thought we needed as children? What if in reclaiming it for ourselves, we not only gifted ourselves but, more importantly, served life? The hurts shaped our people skills, and hopefully will guide us toward becoming more compassionate and loving beings. This is our calling.

It is as though we were a sterling silver ball that had been thrown into the sea of life, where we collected layer upon layer of corrosive rust. Unfortunately, these layers obscured our essential self and our purpose in life. The game of life is to remove the rust and to reclaim our wholeness, our godliness.

So, as you work through your Triangles, you might find a need, from time to time, to go back and change some of your answers for the gifts, hurts, and coping skills. Your new responses do not diminish or negate your original choices. Your new answers simply reveal the next layer of "corrosion" to be healed.

The Family Triangles process offers you one way to remove some of the unconscious layers and to rediscover your calling. In such a context you can serve life consciously, by co-creating with life in life. This is right action; it is living life mindfully.

All of us have chosen places to live, work, and play, and these choices are partly fashioned by our genetically based interests and preferences.
— Nancy Segal

If our genetic imprint affects our environmental preferences, and if environmental experiences can shape given behaviors, then there may be truth in the mystical belief that we are born to have certain experiences for our specific, unique growth. Life is a school; there are lessons to be learned in every experience.

It's almost as if I chose myself; how I wanted to be, what I wanted to be, what I should look like, what abilities I wanted for life in order to achieve what I set out to do.
— Christopher Millar

Psychologist and author James Hillman writes about the idea that there is "something else" to our development as humans, other than what has been put forth by traditional psychology—a third factor beyond genetics and environment. He uses the metaphor of the acorn that contains the oak: that we are "born with a defining image." This "something else" he calls "the soul's code."* It is a factor closely linked to fate or destiny. We describe it as "the calling."

There is a call for each of us to discover, own, and honor our unique gift to life. Our first tasks are to learn to meet our own unmet needs, to forgive and appreciate our past, and to free ourselves of any attitudes, behavior patterns, and identity constructs that consciously interfere with our calling.

Our calling is often obscured by how we filter information, and the meanings that we make of things. We self-organize our identity and our worldview. As a result, the meanings we give to our childhood experiences affect our ongoing reality, our relationships, and how we love. In this fashion, our psyche has been sculpted. Fortunately, compared to the sculptor's stone, the psyche is far more malleable and far less static.

Recurring memories of our childhood keep us connected to our past and to our family of origin. Our knee-jerk reactions to what we assume is happening in the moment often cause us to reenact old patterns or familiar scenarios from the past. Because we associate the gifts of childhood with the hurts, we make the assumption that love

---

*James Hillman, *The Soul's Code*.

cannot be trusted, that life is painful. To deal with current situations we may reach into our worn bag of coping skills. We don't realize that the tools we automatically and habitually turn to will often recreate our childhood hurts!

Habitual behaviors can prevent us from feeling, loving, and seeing the present with an open beginner's mind. Our old reactions limit our ability to give and to receive love, to achieve true intimacy. We become trapped in an old reality, numb to the gift of life and blind to the signposts that point to our calling.

Hidden behind the facade of our personal profile are the unmet needs of childhood: our expectations, our blame, and our shame. This self-portrait can limit and distort our perceptions of others, of ourselves, and of life. From behind this facade, we cannot see the many faces of our love.

Twelve Keys to Seeing Life through New Eyes

In the course of this book, we describe a process of self-discovery; to facilitate your own process, we recommend the following twelve keys to seeing your life through new eyes.

1. Allow yourself to feel and experience what is happening in the moment, to become aware of yourself through self-observation.

2. Stop coping in habitual ways. Begin to change old patterns. Be creative.

3. See apparent incongruities—such as between gifts and hurts, or love and pain—as separate but not contradictory or paradoxical events. This lets you appreciate the possibility that these different events can be connected in time and space and yet, more often than not, separate in terms of significance and implication.

   Try not to create a fixed meaning out of paradox. Live uncertainty into the answer.

4. Stay with the discomfort of moving past old meanings and reactions to life's new experiences.

5. Acknowledge your unmet needs and meet them for yourself, as you would for your best friend. Be your own best friend. Perhaps your greatest calling is to meet your own unmet needs. Perhaps they were purposefully not met in order that you might begin the journey of reclamation. It is often the crack in our psyche that lets in the light.

6. Face your shadow, reclaim your disowned parts, and discover all the hidden faces of love. It is essential to bring your most cherished gift into balance with its opposite. It is also important to realize that the hidden gifts within the hurts can become addictions and obstacles to intimacy.

7. Find security in both aloneness and togetherness. This will give you choice: the choice to react in an old manner, which at times may be appropriate, or to opt for a new and different response.

8. Offer yourself in service to others, not out of fear or the need for approval, but from the outpouring of a heart in overflow, from the fullness of having met your own emotional needs.

9. Begin to live in partnership, seeing yourself as a mirror—not only with your mate, but with all of life. We were all born dependent, and must live in continuing interdependency. With renewed awareness, dependency is no longer seen as weakness, but as an opportunity for shared joy, intimacy, healing, and interconnectedness. Co-create with life in life.

10. Breathe! Allow both pain and joy in and out as rapidly as possible. To cling to either joy or pain creates suffering. Breathe deeply, feel what it is to be human, and watch for the moment-to-moment clues that lead you to the next step in the journey of life. Life is a treasure hunt.

11. Practice "outrageous containment." To be outrageously contained is to feel as if life experiences were created just for you. Live your InSights. It is a balance between radical aliveness and healthy boundaries, between living in joy and living with compassion.

12. Create and sustain an attitude of gratitude (or, as we like to call it, "great fullness"). Gratitude is the key that opens the door to the heart.

Once you begin to practice these ways of being, the signposts that point the way toward your unique gift to life, your calling, will start to become more evident. Remember: *Life meets you where you are.*

When you have begun seeing through new eyes, it might still appear to others that nothing about you has changed. However, you know inside yourself that everything has changed. A Zen proverb says: Before enlightenment, chop wood, carry water; after enlightenment, chop wood, carry water.

There is even more to life than enlightenment. Life is process. Life is purpose. Life is service. Life is play. Life is painful. Life is joyful. We are a "work in progress." Today's solutions can easily become tomorrow's problems.

The power of the Family Triangles process lies not in the specific information revealed at any given time, but in the process itself. Allow it to keep revealing itself to you. It offers a key, a map for exploring new territory, a way of resolving recurring problems and of creating new possibilities for change. Your willingness to enter into and stay with this ongoing process called "life" is a testimony to your nobility and courage as a human being.

Finally, if our genetic imprint affects our environmental preferences, and if environmental experiences can shape our given behaviors, then by becoming fully conscious, we have the choice to live what Carl Rogers called the "good life," which is "a process, not a state of being . . .

a direction, not a destination . . . when there is psychological freedom to move in *any* direction."*

Here's to the good life!

With the drawing of this Love and the voice of this Calling

We shall not cease from exploration
And the end of all our exploring
Will be to arrive where we started
And know the place for the first time.

—T. S. Eliot

---

*Rogers, *On Becoming a Person*.

The Quest

You ask: Who am I?
The Wise One says: Everyone and no one.

You ask: What should I do?
The Wise One says: Live fully.

You ask: How shall I live?
The Wise One says: Love the moment.

You ask: When?
The Wise One says: The only when is now.

You ask: Where?
The Wise One says: The only where is here.

You ask: What do I need?
The Wise One says: Courage, faith, and gratitude.

You ask: What shall I say?
The Wise One says: Say "yes" to Life;
say "I don't know!" to the Mystery;
say "Thank you!" to the All.

You ask: For what shall I be thankful?
The Wise One says: For being who you are.

You ask: Who am I?

— Donna Martin

TEAR HERE

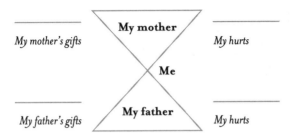

My mother's gifts ——— **My mother** ——— My hurts

Me

My father's gifts ——— **My father** ——— My hurts

**My   My   My People
Gifts   Copes   Skills**

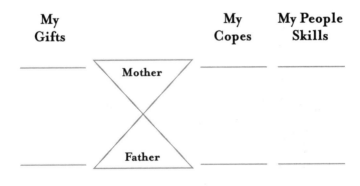

Mother

Father

My Self Portrait

RX—GIVE YOURSELF YOUR PEOPLE SKILLS

Save or tear off for placement on refrigerator

Appendix

List of Gifts, Hurts and Unmet Needs, and Coping Skills

The following are only a few of the possibilities for gifts, unmet needs, and coping skills. They give you some idea of what your answers might be.

Gifts

belonging, wisdom, sensitivity, contentment, security, gentleness, affection, tenderness, generosity, warmth, humor, understanding, acceptance, listening, stability, constancy, integrity, independence, spirituality, determination, creativity, logic, intellect, intuition, openness, consideration, mystery, passion, peacefulness, playfulness, joy, *joie de vivre*, love of nature, common sense, dedication, intelligence, friendliness, social graces, class, ambition, honesty, appreciation, inventiveness, ingenuity, feeling, trust, courage, spontaneity, freedom, discipline, compassion,

kindness, excitement, perseverance, guidance,
nurturing, feeling special, significance,
helpfulness, love of music

Hurts and Unmet Needs

criticism, distance, not seen, not there,
embarrassment, nonacceptance, lack of
attention, disbelief, smothering, insensitivity,
demanding, withdrawn, judgmentalism, lack
of play, nagging, unreliability, excessive
responsibility, unrealistic expectations, lack of
involvement, belittling, lack of validation,
controlling, lack of protection, detachment,
inconsistency, lack of touch, inappropriate touch,
lack of confidence, lack of acknowledgment, lack
of respect, not listening, uncommunicativeness

Coping Skills

independence, self-reliance, self-sufficiency;
pleasing, helpful, mediating, caretaking,
    cooperating;
sensitive, listening, intuitive, attentive,
    introspective, quiet;
achiever, competitive, rational, determined,
    perseverant, goal-oriented;
confrontational, rebellious, nonconformist,
    performer, attention-getter;
sociable, friendly, sense of humor, finding allies;
withdrawal, avoidance, invisible, hiding,
    unassuming;
creativity, love of nature (outdoors), keeping
    busy, physical activity

Triangles Summary

1. My mother's gift:

2. My father's gift:

3. My hurt/unmet need from my mother:

4. My hurt/unmet need from my father:

5. My definition of love:

6. My source of distrust:

7. I feel victimized when:

8. I bonded/fused with:

9. I feel guilty when:

10. I blame others for:

11. I'm addicted to my gifts of:

12. My pain-relief addictions:

13. My seducer style:

14. My rejector style:

15. My coping response to my mother:

16. My coping response to my father:

17. My mask of approval (self-image):

18. My shadow qualitites:

19. My self-repair skills:

About the Authors

PAUL BRENNER: I took a sabbatical in 1976 from the academic and clinical practice of obstetrics, gynecology, and female oncology, to explore other approaches to health and illness. However, for some unknown reason, people with life-threatening illnesses began to call me at home, seeking counseling. I began by seeing one person per day.

No longer restricted by full waiting rooms or the pressures of an impending surgery or delivery, this new format heightened my awareness of personal human factors related to health and illness. These open-ended counseling sessions were held in my home or garden, and allowed ample time for people to talk about their life stories.

During these sessions, which sometimes lasted six to eight hours, patients became my friends. Paradoxically, these new friends often became healers who touched deep forgotten wounds within me. Each brought me closer to the meaning of the wounded healer. I discovered that the ill are an untapped resource for teaching us about health and healing.

These most patient friends became my mirrors. In time, I began to understand the interconnectedness that links all humanity. I realized that the patient-doctor relationship is a reciprocal one in which each is simultaneously serving the other.

As these people shared their lives, I often saw previously unacknowledged parts of myself. Their parents, their families, their loves, their pain, were similar (and at times identical) to mine. The major portion of each session was devoted to unraveling unfinished business. The most common source of unfinished business was found in close personal relationships. Illness offers a forceful reminder to reassess life and its priorities.

Most of those I listened to had been labeled "terminal." Yet they tended to communicate freely about their innermost joys, fears, loves, and sorrows. They reminded me of Kris Kristofferson's words: "Freedom's just another word for nothin' left to lose." There is often an uncommon freedom in the dying person, as the veils that usually obscure the awareness of what really matters fall away.

I met young cancer patients in their twenties and thirties whose birth and formative years took place in chaotic family environments and who, at an early age, had begun to reenact their parents' scenarios. I met numerous older folks who still carried the frustration and the anger of their parents' disharmonious relationships, especially when their own intimate personal lives were shrouded in unresolved conflict.

I realized that familiar, unpleasant childhoods, like worn clothing, were handed down from generation to generation. It was as if these tattered garments were in search of repair; and as if, in reparation, all those who previously had worn the garments would be healed, as well as those yet unborn.

I came to believe that we create our own universe; but the universe we create filters down through our inherited ancestry. Our unique experiences offer each of us a chance to heal both ourselves and what the Hopi refer to as "the long body"—our ancestry. We inherit life's problems from our forefathers and mothers; yet the solutions can be found today. It seems that the resolution of our family conflicts may be the most important factor in healing our psyche and soul, in helping us to live out the fullness of life, and in the acceptance of death.

I once worked with a sixty-eight-year-old woman who was dying from cancer that was considered "untreatable." In our first session, she was frail and could hardly breathe to speak. When she did respond, she spoke only in anger, and only about her mother who had died thirty years before. She blamed her mother as the cause of her illness, her unhappy marriage, and even the problems she experienced with her daughter.

Finally, resting with her eyes closed, she seemed to enter a trance state. This was followed by sudden, uncontrollable weeping. She was remembering herself at age sixteen, sitting in her Brooklyn tenement kitchen, crying. She had just broken up with her first love. Her mother entered the room and quietly placed her hand on her daughter's head, saying tenderly, "*meine kinde, meine kinde*, it will be all right . . . it will be all right." In that moment of recall, she screamed, "My God, she did love me! My mother loved me!" Her outer demeanor changed as she suddenly felt free of all her emotional pain.

When she returned the following week, she appeared completely changed. She began by saying, "Although I have lived in San Diego for over thirty years, I never purposefully watched the sunset or reflected on the wonderment of my own existence. I was too busy. After last week, I now awake early in the morning, walk the beaches, and have a different relationship with my husband. I cherish each moment. I have become spellbound, mesmerized by sunsets and birdsongs. I find myself finally at peace."

Six months later, after this profound rebirth, my friend died. But I feel that she died in health, not in sickness. From this and other similar experiences, health, for me, has come to mean the appreciation and acceptance of life. I could not help but wonder: Do I need terminal illness to force myself to finish my own unfinished emotional business? Can I remove the veils, while I'm still healthy, that obscure my awareness of what's really important? My patients were teachers who taught me that health is not necessarily the absence of disease. Perhaps most importantly, they taught me the nobility of what it is to be human. Needless to say, I left my medical practice and entered the field of psychotherapy.

Over the subsequent years, with Donna Martin, I developed the process of Family Triangles to incorporate what my patients taught me. This is a process based not on blame but on insight, appreciation, and forgiveness; a process for seeing life, oneself, one's family, and others, through new eyes.

DONNA MARTIN: My personal journey began as the oldest of five children in a very loving Canadian family. The more I work with people who've been severely traumatized, the more I am aware of how blessed I've been. What I received as gifts from my childhood were an unquestionable sense of security and an appreciation for life and for people. My parents instilled in me a basic trust that continues to be the ground of my psychological and spiritual way of being. It also permeates and informs my style of working as a therapist.

My professional life journey moved, in a very nonlinear way, from teaching school to teaching yoga and meditation, to relaxation and stress management, to counseling and working with addictions, to psychotherapy and the Hakomi Method, to training therapists. Along the way, I met Paul Brenner at a Canadian Holistic Medical Association (CHMA) conference. I had gone especially to hear him speak; that meeting changed my life. Here was a man who lived with a passionate commitment to authenticity and truth; a man who was ready to give up material success to pursue his ideals; a man who demonstrated a trust in the wisdom of the body that others only talked about.

Paul Brenner uses a method in his talks and workshops that he calls "silent communication." He shows us that we have an inner knowing that can be accessed if we trust it enough. He also shows us that our lives are inextricably interconnected and that healing is a two-way process. The distinctions between giving and receiving, between being the healer and being healed, began to fall away as I watched him work.

I invited Paul to do workshops in Canada, and a strong friendship and working partnership developed. When the Family Triangles process was born, it took on a life of its own that forged our connection as it unfolded. Over the years, we have worked with this amazing process both together and separately, in our personal lives as well as with clients and in workshops. It has become the basis of my understanding of psychology and of the connection between nature, nurture, and our spiritual life.

We have discovered, with Family Triangles, the unity of a person's history and calling in life. Along with that discovery and others, we have become convinced of the perfect order found in life's journey, of the wholeness of things as they are.

References

Introduction

xi: Marcel Proust, *Remembrance Of Things Past*, trans. C. K. Scott-Moncrief (New York: Random House, 1934).

xiii: Anaïs Nin. (Though the precise location or occasion of this statement could not be identified, it is commonly attributed to Anaïs Nin.)

Chapter One: Family Triangles

1: Jalal al-Din Rumi, *The Essential Rumi*, trans. Coleman Barks (San Francisco: HarperCollins, 1995), 142.

7: T. S. Eliot, "Little Gidding," *Four Quartets* (New York: Harcourt Brace, 1971), 55.

Chapter Two: Gifts

9: *The Essential Rumi*, 281.

9: James Kagen, "Temperament," in *Handbook of Child and Adolescent Psychiatry*, ed. Joseph Noshpitz et al. (New York: John Wiley & Sons, 1996); Robert Karen,

Becoming Attached: First Relationships and How They Shape Our Capacity to Love (New York: Oxford University Press, 1998); Nancy Segal, *Entwined Lives: Twins and What They Tell Us About Human Behavior* (New York: Dutton, 1999).

14: Jean Piaget, "The Growth of Logical Thinking," *The Essential Piaget* (New York: Harper, 1977), 405–44.

16: Stella Chess and Alexander Thomas, *Origins and Evolution of Behavior Disorders* (Cambridge, Mass.: Harvard University Press, 1987); Segal, *Entwined Lives*.

19: Harry Stack Sullivan, *Conceptions of Modern Psychiatry* (New York: Norton, 1940), 22.

22: Joan Riviere and Melanie Klein, *Love, Hate, and Reparation* (New York: Norton, 1964), 19.

28: Robert Assagioli, *Psychosynthesis* (New York: Penguin Books, 1972), 22.

33: Carl Jung, *The Undiscovered Self* (New York: New American Library, 1957).

34: R. D. Laing, *Self and Others* (Harmondsworth, England: Pelican, 1971), 127.

35: Ron Kurtz, *Body-Centered Psychotherapy: The Hakomi Method* (Mendocino, Calif.: LifeRhythm, 1990), 32–33.

39: Nikos Kazantzakis, *The Saviors of God: Spiritual Exercises*, trans. Kimon Friar (New York: Simon & Schuster, 1960), 19.

39: Jay Greenberg and Stephen Mitchell, *Object Relations in Psychoanalytic Theory* (Cambridge, Mass.: Harvard University Press, 1983), 23.

40: *The Essential Rumi*, 3.

Chapter Three: Hurts

41: *The Essential Rumi*, 281.

44: Harville Hendrix, *Getting the Love You Want: A Guide for Couples* (New York: Harper & Row, 1988), 15.

45: Thomas Moore, *Care of the Soul* (New York: HarperCollins, 1992), 166.

46: Riviere and Klein, *Love, Hate, and Reparation*, 67.

47: John Bradshaw, *Healing the Shame that Binds You* (New York: Health Communications, 1988).

48: Riviere and Klein, *Love, Hate, and Reparation*, 66.

56: Gerald Jampolsky, *Good-bye to Guilt* (New York: Bantam, 1985), 31.

57: Abraham H. Maslow, *The Farther Reaches of Human Nature* (New York: Penguin, 1993), 39.

60: Melanie Klein, *Psychoanalysis of Children* (London: Hogarth, 1932), 184. (Klein was a student of Freud; she discusses the idea of internalized parents.)

63: Carl Rogers, *On Becoming a Person: A Therapist's View of Psychotherapy* (Boston: Houghton Mifflin, 1961), 184–96.

70;71: Abraham H. Maslow, *Toward a Psychology of Being*, 2d ed. (New York: Van Nostrand Reinhold, 1968), 202; 211.

73: Wayne Muller, *Legacy of the Heart: The Spiritual Advantages of a Painful Childhood* (New York: Simon & Schuster, 1992), 2.

74: Riviere and Klein, *Love, Hate, and Reparation*, 18.

75: Karen, *Becoming Attached*.

75: Maslow, *Toward a Psychology of Being*, 8.

CHAPTER FOUR: FROM RELATIONSHIP
TO PARTNERSHIP

77: Jalal al-Din Rumi, *Feeling the Shoulder of the Lion*, trans. Coleman Barks (Putney, Vt.: Threshold Books, 1991), 48.

79: Clark Moustakas, *Loneliness and Love* (Englewood Cliffs, N.J.: Prentice-Hall, 1972), 145.

87: Sullivan, *Conceptions of Modern Psychiatry*, 10.

87: Paul Brenner, R. Livingston, and J. Weeks, "Chronic Pain and Its Management" (Paper delivered at the Annual Meeting of the American Society for the Study of Pain, 1977).

89: Maslow, *Toward a Psychology of Being*, 16.

89: Baruch Spinoza, *Ethics* (New York: White and Guttmann, 1953).

91: John Welwood, *Journey of the Heart* (New York: HarperCollins, 1990), 89.

98: Gay and Kathlyn Hendricks, *Conscious Loving: The Journey to Co-commitment* (New York: Bantam, 1990), 7.

104: Hermann Hesse, *Wandering: Notes and Sketches*, trans. James Wright (New York: Farrar, Strauss, and Giroux, 1972), 7.

105: Thomas Merton, *The New Man* (New York: Bantam, 1981), 39.

106: David Schnarch, *Passionate Marriage: Love, Sex, and Intimacy in Emotionally Committed Relationships* (New York: Norton, 1997), 51.

CHAPTER FIVE: PAIN, FEAR, AND COPING

107: Jalal al-Din Rumi, *The Illuminated Rumi*, trans. Coleman Barks (New York: Broadway Books, 1997), 40.

112: Jerome Kagan, *The Nature of the Child* (New York: BasicBooks, 1984), 6.

115: Karen, *Becoming Attached*, 226.

115–116: Maslow, *Toward a Psychology of Being*, 51; 52.

122: Carl Jung, *Memories, Dreams, Reflections* (New York: Vintage, 1989), 171.

123: Maslow, *Toward a Psychology of Being*, 16; 142.

124: Jalal al-Din Rumi, *Like This*, trans. Coleman Barks (Athens, Ga.: Maypop, 1990), 45.

124: Jung, *The Undiscovered Self*, 95.

125: Assagioli, *Psychosynthesis*, 22.

125: Christina and Stanislav Grof, *The Stormy Search for the Self: A Guide to Personal Growth through Transformational Crisis* (New York: Tarcher/Putnam, 1990), 106.

126: Alcoholics Anonymous World Services, *Alcoholics Anonymous* ("Big Book"), 3d ed. (New York: AA, 1976), 58–59.

134: Helen Palmer, *The Enneagram: Understanding Yourself and the Others in Your Life* (New York: HarperCollins, 1988), 389.

134: Lawrence LeShan, *Cancer as a Turning Point* (New York: Dutton, 1989); David Spiegel, *Living Beyond Limits* (New York: Times Books, 1993); Dean Ornish, *Dr. Dean Ornish's Program for Reversing Heart Disease* (New York: Random House, 1988).

135: Susan Sontag, *Illness as Metaphor; and, AIDS and Its Metaphors* (New York: Doubleday, 1990).

138: Maslow, *Toward a Psychology of Being*, 47.

139: Jung, *Memories, Dreams, Reflections*, 237.

139: Hal Stone and Sidra Winkelman, *Embracing Heaven & Earth: A Personal Odyssey* (Marina del Ray, Calif.: Devorss, 1985); Richard Schwartz, *Internal Family Systems Therapy* (New York: Guilford Press, 1995); Ron Kurtz, *Body-Centered Psychotherapy*; Erving and Miriam Polster, *Gestalt Therapy Integrated* (New York: Vintage Books, 1974).

140: *The Enlightened Mind: An Anthology of Sacred Prose*, ed. Stephen Mitchell (New York: HarperCollins, 1991), 3. (The Upanishads are ancient texts that form a part of Hindu scripture.)

CHAPTER SIX: OUR CALLING

141: *The Essential Rumi*, 205.

141: Paul Brenner, "The Biologic Origin of the Human Psyche." (Paper presented at the Fourth International Congress on Perinatal Psychology, Amherst, Mass., August 1989, which looks at the story of fertilization, and the behavior of the egg and the sperm, from a mythological perspective.)

143: Segal, *Entwined Lives*, 19.

143: Christopher Millar, quoted in *Primal Connections*, ed. Elizabeth Noble (New York: Simon & Schuster, 1993), 148.

144: James Hillman, *The Soul's Code* (New York: Warner, 1996). (See the chapter entitled "Neither Nature nor Nurture—Something Else.")

149: Rogers, *On Becoming a Person*, 186–87.

149: Eliot, *Four Quartets*, 59.

OTHER BOOKS FROM
BEYOND WORDS PUBLISHING, INC.

FORGIVENESS
The Greatest Healer of All
Author: Gerald G. Jampolsky, M.D.
Foreword: Neale Donald Walsch
$12.95, softcover

Forgiveness: The Greatest Healer of All is written in simple, down-to-earth language. It explains why so many of us find it difficult to forgive and why holding on to grievances is really a decision to suffer. The book describes what causes us to be unforgiving and how our minds work to justify this. It goes on to point out the toxic side effects of being unforgiving and the havoc it can play on our bodies and on our lives. But above all, it leads us to the vast benefits of forgiving.

The author shares powerful stories that open our hearts to the miracles which can take place when we truly believe that no one needs to be excluded from our love. Sprinkled throughout the book are Forgiveness Reminders that may be used as daily affirmations supporting a new life free of past grievances.

TEACH ONLY LOVE
The Twelve Principles of Attitudinal Healing
Author: Gerald G. Jampolsky, M.D.
$12.95, softcover

From best-selling author Dr. Gerald Jampolsky comes a revised and expanded version of one of his classic works, based on *A Course in Miracles*. In 1975, Dr. Jampolsky founded the Center for Attitudinal Healing, a place where children and adults with life-threatening illnesses could practice peace of mind as an instrument of spiritual transformation and inner healing—practices that soon evolved into an approach to life with profound benefits for everyone. This book explains the twelve principles developed at the Center, all of which are based on the healing power of love, forgiveness, and oneness. They provide a powerful guide that allows all of us to heal our relationships and bring peace and harmony to every aspect of our lives.

OUR TURN, OUR TIME
Women Truly Coming of Age
Editor: Cynthia Black; Foreword: Christina Baldwin
$14.95, softcover

Our Turn, Our Time is an amazing collection of essays written by women who are committed to celebrating and valuing their passages into the second half of life. These women are redefining the role older women play in contemporary society by embracing creativity, spirituality, and sisterhood. These essays are filled with insight, humor, and compassion on a broad variety of topics: the richness of women's groups, the rewards of volunteering, the power of crone ceremonies, the fires of creative expression, the challenges of a changing body, and the confidence that comes from success in later life.

EVERY DAY GOD
Heart to Heart with the Divine
Authors: David and Takeko Hose
$14.95, softcover

When Takeko Hose was accidentally shot and paralyzed from the knees down, she and her husband, David, reached out desperately for divine assistance through a succession of what David calls "naked prayers." *Every Day God* is the record of a remarkable communication between authors David and Takeko and God. Not a stickler for ritual, a lofty voice from beyond, or an enigma, their God is a warm and

caring parent, eager to nurture and love uncondi-
tionally all of His children. Comforting and enlight-
ening, the teachings in *Every Day God* are lighthearted,
often humorous, and relevant to modern life. And at
the core of each teaching is an invitation to meet this
largely undiscovered self within our innermost
hearts, a self that flows from our divine source.

THE INTUITIVE WAY
A Guide to Living from Inner Wisdom
Author: Penney Peirce; Foreword: Carol Adrienne
$16.95, softcover

When intuition is in full bloom, life takes on a
magical, effortless quality; your world is suddenly full
of synchronicities, creative insights, and abundant
knowledge just for the asking. *The Intuitive Way* shows
you how to enter that state of perceptual aliveness and
integrate it into daily life to achieve greater natural
flow through an easy-to-understand, ten-step
course. Author Penney Peirce synthesizes teachings
from psychology, East-West philosophy, religion,
metaphysics, and business. In simple and direct language, Peirce describes the intuitive process as a new
way of life and demonstrates many practical applica-
tions from speeding decision-making to expanding
personal growth. Whether you're just beginning to
search for a richer, fuller life experience or are looking for more subtle, sophisticated insights about your
spiritual path, *The Intuitive Way* will be your compan-
ion as you progress through the stages of intuition
development.

THE WOMAN'S BOOK OF DREAMS
Dreaming as a Spiritual Practice
Author: Connie Cockrell Kaplan
Foreword: Jamie Sams
$14.95, softcover

Dreams are the windows to your future and the catalysts to bringing the new and creative into your life. Everyone dreams. Understanding the power of dreaming helps you achieve your greatest potential with ease. *The Woman's Book of Dreams* emphasizes the uniqueness of women's dreaming and shows the reader how to dream with intention, clarity, and focus. In addition, this book will teach you how to recognize the thirteen types of dreams, how your monthly cycles affect your dreaming, how the moon's position in the sky and its relationship to your astrological chart determine your dreaming, and how to track your dreams and create a personal map of your dreaming patterns. Connie Kaplan guides you through an ancient woman's group form called dream circle—a sacred space in which to share dreams with others on a regular basis. Dream circle allows you to experience life's mystery by connecting with other dreamers. It shows you that through dreaming together with your circle, you create the reality in which you live. It is time for you to recognize the power of dreams and to put yours into action. This book will inspire you to do all that—and more.

QUESTIONS FOR MY FATHER
Finding the Man Behind Your Dad
Author: Vin Staniforth
$15.00, hardcover

Questions for My Father is a little book that asks big questions—some serious, some playful, some risky. Each question is an opportunity to open, rejuvenate, or bring closure to the powerful but often overlooked relationship between fathers and children. Fathers have long been regarded as objects of mystery and fascination. *Questions for My Father* provides a blueprint for uncovering the full dimensions of the man behind the mystery. It offers a way to let fathers tell their personal stories and to let children explore their own knowledge and understanding of one of the largest figures in their lives. In rediscovering their dad, readers will discover themselves.

RITES OF PASSAGE
Celebrating Life's Changes
Authors: Kathleen Wall, Ph.D., and Gary Ferguson
$12.95, softcover

Every major transition in our lives—be it marriage, high-school graduation, the death of a parent or spouse, or the last child leaving home—brings with it opportunities for growth and self-actualization and for repositioning ourselves in the world. Personal ritual—the focus of *Rites of Passage*—allows us to use the energy held within the anxiety of change to nourish the new person that is forever struggling to be born. *Rites of Passage* begins by explaining to readers that human growth is not linear, as many of us assume, but rather occurs in a five-part cycle. After sharing the patterns of transition, the authors then show the reader how ritual can help him or her move through these specific life changes: work and career, intimate relationships, friends, divorce, changes within the family, adolescence, issues in the last half of life, and personal loss.

CREATE YOUR OWN LOVE STORY

The Art of Lasting Relationships
Author: David W. McMillan, Ph.D.; Foreword: John Gray, Ph.D.
$21.95, hardcover; $14.95, softcover

Create Your Own Love Story breaks new ground in the crowded and popular field of relationship self-help guides. *Create Your Own Love Story* is based on a four-part model—Spirit, Trust, Trade, and Art—derived from McMillan's twenty years' work in community theory and clinical psychology. Each of these four elements is divided into short, highly readable chapters that include both touching and hilarious examples from real marriages, brief exercises based on visualization and journal writing that are effective whether used by one or both partners, and dialogues readers can have with themselves and/or their partners. This book shows readers how they can use their own energy and initiative, with McMillan's help, to make their marriage stronger, more enduring, and more soul-satisfying.

LOVE SWEETER LOVE

Creating Relationships of Simplicity and Spirit
Author: Jann Mitchell; Foreword: Susan Jeffers
$12.95, softcover

How do we find the time to nurture relationships with the people we love? By simplifying. And *Love Sweeter Love* teaches us how to decide who and what is most important, how to work together as a couple, and how to savor life's sweetest moments. Mitchell has warm, practical, easy-to-understand advice for everyone—young, mature, single, married, or divorced—interested in creating simple, sacred time for love.

To order or to request a catalog, contact
Beyond Words Publishing, Inc.
20827 N.W. Cornell Road, Suite 500
Hillsboro, OR 97124-9808
503-531-8700 or 1-800-284-9673

You can also visit our Web site at *www.beyondword.com*
or e-mail us at *info@beyondword.com.*

Paul Brenner and Donna Martin are available
for lectures and workshops.

E-mail: brenners@familytriangles.com
insight@donnamartin.net

Websites: www.familytriangles.com
www.donnamartin.net

Call Paul Brenner at 909-659-4827
Donna Martin at 250-374-2514
fax Paul Brenner at 909-659-9886

BEYOND WORDS PUBLISHING, INC.

OUR CORPORATE MISSION:

Inspire to Integrity

OUR DECLARED VALUES:

We give to all of life as life has given us.
We honor all relationships.
Trust and stewardship are integral to fulfilling dreams.
Collaboration is essential to create miracles.
Creativity and aesthetics nourish the soul.
Unlimited thinking is fundamental.
Living your passion is vital.
Joy and humor open our hearts to growth.
It is important to remind ourselves of love.